# Workbook

## For

**Oprah Winfrey and Dr. Bruce Perry's**

# What Happened To You

## Conversations on Trauma, Resilience and Healing

Genie Reads

# Table of Contents

*To the folks who form the "We"*

# Foreword

A black child was frequently whipped for the smallest of things and then told to wipe any trace of sadness off her face. In the rural South where this kid was being raised, this was a common practice.

A pattern of forceful compliance and traumatized early life affected this child's relationships, decisions and interactions in the next four decades of her life.

As you might imagine, she grew up to become a people pleaser. A better part of her life was shaped by what she had endured at the hands of the very people who were supposed to be her caregivers.

In 1989, a young academic child psychiatrist was studying the impact of early stress and trauma on brain development. His work wasn't well-known at the time; childhood trauma was a topic that was rarely on the radar of most of his peers.

But it was on someone's radar.

One fine day, to his utter surprise, the young enthusiast receives a call from Oprah Winfrey. Yes, the same Oprah Winfrey from the Oprah Winfrey Show; the same innocent black child who had grown up suffering from trauma inflicted by her caregivers in the name of love.

Deeply interested in the subject, Oprah wanted to talk about childhood trauma and its effects on early brain development with the young neuroscientist, Dr. Bruce D Perry. But that was just the beginning of a long journey to understand how our miraculous brains are shaped by trauma experienced early in life.

The meaningful conversations that began after that first meeting in 1989 led to many great things; the 1991 drafting of the National Child Protection Act, the passing of the 'Oprah Bill' in 1993 and the establishment of the Oprah Winfrey Leadership Academy for Girls (OWLAG) in 2007.

As for the conversations themselves, they continued through The Oprah Winfrey Show and other platforms, raising great awareness about childhood trauma and its effects on early brain development.

Having had firsthand experience with childhood trauma herself, the subject was extremely close to Oprah's heart. It's no wonder then that trauma-related topics, be it maltreatment, sexual abuse or false imprisonment, have been the gist of her shows for nearly twenty-five years.

And for more than thirty years, she has had deep conversations about trauma, brain, resilience and healing with Dr. Bruce D Perry.

Conversations that led to some very important conclusions as to how our brain, and therefore our personalities, are shaped by *What Happened to Us*. Not *What's Wrong With Us*.

Our failed attempts at leading a life of our dreams, to understand ourselves or those around us or to feel more balanced, nourished or secure is an indication that it's time. It's time to explore our trauma, pull those wounds out, accept them and heal from them. All while becoming more wise and more empathic.

And that is where this workbook can be of groundbreaking value to you and those around you.

It not only explains the gist of those important conversations between Oprah Winfrey and Dr. Bruce D Perry about the impact of childhood trauma and adversity, it also includes thought provoking questions and exercises at the end of each chapter to help you explore and make sense of your own trauma. And heal from it.

The best part about this workbook is that it doesn't require you to go public with your pain. Although it is highly recommended that you get professional help when needed, the questions and exercises in this workbook can help you probe into those painful wounds privately and on your own time.

So don't feel pressured to complete all the exercises at once or answer all questions immediately after reading a chapter. Take as long as you want to think about what you've learnt and how it can help you explore *What Happened to You*.

But that's not all. As you'll also learn in this workbook, it's possible to heal from trauma and come out of it as a wiser person. The exercises within, therefore, will also help guide you on the path to healing and a better future.

And lastly...

Try to be as open and honest as you can about the questions and exercises in this workbook. Remember, this workbook is yours to keep forever. No one can see what you answered to a particular question. So be as candid as you can and use it as a tool to explore your own thoughts, experiences, beliefs and actions.

Most importantly, use it to explore your own trauma.

Because while taking a deeper look at What Happened to You can't change the past, it certainly has the potential to change your future for the better.

And we all want a better future, don't we?

# Chapter One – Making Sense of The World

## Summary

A newborn doesn't come into this world questioning their self-worth; they don't really think *'Am I enough?'*. However, as these little individuals open their eyes and begin to make sense of the world around them, their experiences start to differ.

And unfortunately, they might end up questioning that unwavering self-worth after all.

That's a sad reality of our world.

Not every infant is nestled in the arms of loving parents who just can't seem to get enough of them. Some are also born in broken families that struggle financially. Or raised by an abusive parent who continues the legacy.

And this is how two children, born at the same time to two different families with different circumstances, develop two different worldviews and lead two completely different lives.

Our brain is a complex yet marvelous structure that plays a vital role in shaping who we are. But before that, this magnificent organ is shaped by our life circumstances; all the way from the moment we're born to the day we die.

This is precisely why it makes sense to look at *What Happened to Someone* in order to understand how their brain works and why they function the way they do.

But before we can connect the dots, it's worth taking a deeper look at how our brain is naturally wired.

- Cortex ( Controls Creativity, Values, Thinking, Time, Hope, Language )

- Limbic ( Reward, Memory, Bonding, Emotions )

- Diencephalon ( Arousal, Sleep, Appetite, Movement )

- Brain Stem ( Temperature, Respiration, Cardiac )

This can be aptly called the brain system. The brain develops from the bottom up i.e. from the brainstem up to the diencephalon, limbic and finally the cortex. The brainstem is a more primitive part of the brain controlling mostly regulatory functions such as the breathing, heart rate and body temperature.

The parts at the top are more advanced and therefore capable of more sophisticated functions. They're involved with actions such as speech, language, thinking and planning. They're also the natural warehouses for our beliefs and values.

But all these parts of the brain can't work on their own. They rely on sensory input, aka information about what's happening around us as well as inside us, to perform their specific functions.

All this information first reaches the lower parts of the brain. This means that whenever we experience anything inside or outside our bodies, the primitive part of our brain is engaged before things get sent up to the *smarty pants* i.e. the cortex.

Here's another interesting fact. While the top, *more-brainy* part of the brain (such as cortex) can tell time and distinguish between the past, present and future, the poor brainstem can't. Which is why it's very aptly called the *'lizard brain'*.

Now depending on what you think about lizards, that's a funny name. But just like a lizard isn't capable of planning much and simply lives in the moment, the lizard brain is good at merely reacting to stuff.

Talking about reactions, let's discuss one of Dr. Perry's patients to get an even clearer understanding of how the brain works.

The patient, Mike Roseman, was a Korean war veteran who had classic PTSD symptoms. Having lived through the horrors of a war, Mr. Roseman had seen a lot. So his symptoms had a hard time leaving him alone.

Even after more than thirty years had passed, Mr. Roseman's life was traumatized by PTSD. One particular night, as he was on a date with someone special, Mr. Roseman had a full-blown panic attack in the streets within seconds of hearing a motorcycle backfire.

His date Sally desperately wanted to get some help for him. So they both ended up in Dr. Perry's office looking for some answers. At the time, a young and inexperienced Dr. Perry couldn't think of anything better than to look at Mr. Roseman's situation from the lens of a neuroscientist.

He thought, what was happening in his brain *when that motorcycle backfired?*

And that thought led him to an important conclusion.

Mr. Roseman's brain had adapted to the constant threat and the very real danger he had endured during the Korean war. His brainstem, where all the information from our external and internal environment is first processed, had therefore made memories to protect him from any potential danger in future.

But the poor brainstem can't tell the difference between past, present and future. It couldn't recognize that more than three decades had passed since Mr. Roseman was at war. And since all external signals the brain receives *have* to go through the brainstem first, the cortex had no say in the situation.

At least not yet.

Well, the poor thing is shut down anyway when something stressful happens. Such as that motorcycle backfiring in Mr. Roseman's case.

Anyhow, when the brain finally comes to its senses and the cortex can access this information, it curses the lower parts for ringing a false alarm. Everything comes under control and we all live happily until another false alarm rings.

In Mr. Roseman's case, these false alarms were a routine. But the good news was that once the higher parts of his brain sensed that there was no real danger in the present, he calmed down. It took time, though.

That fateful evening, it took him the whole night to calm down.

As Dr. Perry explained all of this to Mr. Roseman, he couldn't help but feel relieved.

It was clear to him, as it must now be for you, that our brains are hardwired to *act and feel* before thinking. All thanks to the natural sequence of information processing in this powerhouse of ours.

But is it enough to know that all information our brain receives is processed in a certain sequence? Can this fact alone justify how a person thinks, acts and behaves in their daily lives?

The answer is, *not really.*

When trying to understand someone's brain and their behavior, it's also really important to look at the life experiences they've had that led to the unique ways their brain develops and functions.

But how do our experiences shape the brain and affect how it functions?

Good question.

We talked earlier about how a newborn tries to make sense of the world as soon as they open their eyes. One might think that they've just started to absorb everything around them. But, in reality, the process of taking in and storing life experiences in the developing brain begins when they're still in the womb.

Making sense of the world is a complex process that even the researchers don't fully understand yet.

But since it's important to our discussion, here's a tremendously oversimplified version for you.

The brain needs information to make sense of what we're experiencing from both inside and outside our bodies. It's external sources of information include the sensory organs such as eyes, ears, nose and skin. Internally, we have a sensory system called *interoception* that *intercepts* internal signals such as hunger, cold and shortness of breath etc.

Now, this information isn't directly received by the brain. It's the job of brain cells called 'neurons' to carry these messages to the brain which then activates the relevant systems to deal with *the problem at hand.* Such as hunger, thirst, danger etc.

This process is continuous i.e. the brain keeps receiving information from inside and outside sources.

It then categorizes this information and sends it up the 'brain system' for further processing. This categorization isn't just random though. The brain sorts information based on certain criteria. So, for instance, if it receives some visual input from the eyes along with some information from the nose at *the same time* (think you've just seen a wonderfully smelling steak!), it sorts that information together and sends it higher up the brain. These sensations of sight and smell from the same experience then connect together to form memories.

What we now have is a full-fledged experience that is stored in our brain in the form of a memory. This catalog of memories keeps expanding. It not only helps us make sense of what's happening around us, but also shapes our worldview.

Now, brain development is all fired up in a fetus which is making as much as 20,000 new neurons each second. That makes sense. They're in a brand new world so their brain is actively making new connections to make sense of this strange new place.

But this also implies that the young ones are like sponges, absorbing so much more than we care to think. They don't yet understand the words adults speak, but are extremely sensitive to non-verbal cues and the emotional tone of their environment.

But a young child doesn't have a fully developed cortex. They also don't have the ability to form a precise memory that clearly describes *the what, when, how, who, or where.* But they can still make and store memories in the lower parts of the brain that have already developed.


So if a child experiences trauma or abuse at a young age, they can still remember it. But their brain can make certain associations that can cause confusion for years to come.

That's because the young brain has formed an imprecise memory of that traumatic or abusive incident. It can't exactly recall who did it, when they did it or how it happened. It just knows that, for instance, the person abusing them had a certain hair color or the place had red ambient lighting. Later in their lives, when such a child finds themselves in a place where any of these hints are present, they might have a full-blown panic attack for no apparent reason.

A history of abuse at a young age can also cause something known as *'poisoned intimacy'*. Those affected have a hard time setting boundaries and saying *'No'*. They become *'people pleasers'* like Oprah.

But trauma isn't just limited to sexual abuse or poisoned intimacy. It also presents itself in other traumatic life events such as the divorce of parents. Divorce has a drastic impact on a child's self-worth, particularly when they don't feel respected by the decision of their parents.

The younger a child, the more undeveloped their brain is, and the more they are affected by trauma, adversity and abuse.

It affects how they think, behave and act. It impacts the values and believes that they hold true. And it shapes how they view the world around them.

In other words...

For better or for worse, *What Happened to You* has the power to shape who you are.

## Lessons

1. We're hardwired to act and feel before thinking.

2. *What Happened to Us* shapes us.

3. Trauma and abuse experienced at a young age can cause lifelong problems.

4. It's no use thinking a child is *too young* to understand. Children can understand everything.

5. Divorce is like death to children.

## Issues To Think About

1. Why are some behaviors hard to unlearn?

   - Question: What was the hardest behavior that you had to unlearn? Why do you think there was a need for you to unlearn this behavior?

   _____

   _____

   _____

   _____

- Question: Recall an incident where you acted before thinking? Did you later realize it would have been better to think before acting? Why?

_____

_____

_____

_____

2. Divorce and its impact on children

- Question: How do you think divorce affects children?

_____

_____

_____

_____

3. Adversity at a young age

- Question: Did you face trauma and adversity at a young age? How do you think it impacted you?

_____

_____

_____

_____

_____

- Question: Do you have a hard time setting boundaries? Do you find it hard to say 'no'? Why do you think it's like that?

_____

_____

_____

_____

## Achieving Targets

1. How can you unlearn some of the adaptive behaviors that no longer serve you?

2. How can you better deal with your own trauma so the children around you aren't affected by it?

3. How can you set good boundaries for yourself? How can you say 'no' when you really don't want to do something?

4. If divorced, how can you create a 'safe' environment for young children and introduce a new partner to them in the best possible way?

## Actionable Movements

1. Complete the following exercise to develop improved coping strategies in face of adversity. This is particularly helpful to unlearn some of the coping mechanisms that no longer serve you and talk yourself out of them

| What's the worry? |
| --- |
|  |

| Worst-case scenario | Most likely scenario |
| --- | --- |
|  |  |

| Chance it'll happen —------% | Chance it'll happen —------% |
|---|---|
| What if it happens?<br><br>Will I be okay in one week?   yes/no<br><br>Will I be okay in one month?  yes/no<br><br>Will I be okay in one year?    yes/no | What if it happens?<br><br>Will I be okay in one week?   yes/no<br><br>Will I be okay in one month?  yes/no<br><br>Will I be okay in one year?    yes/no |

| How do you feel about the worry now? |
|---|
|  |

2. Explore 5 things you're doing in front of your children that may be harming them. Find out what to do instead.

The first one has been done for you as an example.

- I **fight with my partner in front of my children**.
- What to do instead: **I'll try and keep any aggression or bickering with my partner private**.


- I —

  _____

  _____

- What to do instead: —-

  _____

  _____

- I —-

  _____

  _____

- What to do instead: —-

  _____

  _____

- I —-

  _____

  _____

- What to do instead: —-

  _____

  _____

- I —-

  _____

  _____

- What to do instead: —-

  _____

  _____

3. Explore 3 areas in your life where you need to set good boundaries? What do you think you need instead?

**Area #1 —-**_____

I feel _____ when _____ because _____

What I need is _____

**Area #2 —-**_____

I feel _____ when _____ because _____

What I need is _____

**Area #3 —-**_____

I feel _____ when _____ because _____

What I need is _____

4. Included below are 5 tips to build and maintain effective boundaries. In the empty space following each, write down how you'll implement these in your own life.

   The first one includes an example for illustration purposes. Feel free to add your own answer in the additional space provided below.

   - How can you start small with a few boundaries at first and build up from there? You don't need to have a hundred boundaries in place at once.
   - **I'll start with a shared agreement with my partner about dividing the kids' schooling responsibilities. I think I'll take care of helping them with their homework while my partner will pick 'em up and drop them off for school.**

     _____
     _____
     _____
     _____

   - How can you not let 'small' things slide?  letting your boundaries 'slip' can cause confusion and set unrealistic expectations.

     _____
     _____
     _____
     _____

   - How can you add some extras? Sometimes your boundaries may need a little 'top-up'. Don't be shy to do so when need arises.

     _____
     _____
     _____
     _____

- How can you have the right mindset? It's hard to set effective boundaries for yourself when you think you're not worthy of them. Ditch this mindset.

_____
_____
_____
_____

- How can you respect and recognize others' boundaries? If you don't respect someone else's boundaries, they won't respect yours.

_____
_____
_____
_____

5. Included below are 4 aspects of helping children deal with the divorce of a parent. In the empty space following each, write down how you'll tackle these in your own life.

   **(Feel free to fill this section in even if it doesn't apply to you!)**

   - What should we tell our children about our separation/divorce?

_____
_____
_____
_____

   - What can we do to make the transition easier?

_____
_____
_____
_____

   - When should I call a doctor for my child?

_____
_____

_____

_____

- What if there is a more serious problem? Who else can I approach for support and help?

_____

_____

_____

_____

## Checklist

1. Our coping mechanisms can become outdated. They need to be changed to suit our current circumstances.

2. Childhood adversity at a young age can have far-reaching effects.

3. Divorce is like death, not separation, for children.

4. Our brain is naturally wired to react and feel before thinking.

# Chapter Two – Seeking Balance

### Summary

*"What Happened to You?"* should always be the first question to ask…

···whether understanding how and why a person has developed a certain worldview…

···or finding solutions to substance abuse and helping those suffering from addiction..

···or figuring out how and why we sometimes fail to maintain the very balance and rhythm that is critical to survive and thrive…

It all comes down to asking *What Happened to You.*

The answer to which, it seems, our physical self already knows.

Take the heart, for example.

Have you ever felt a sudden fluttering of the heart or sensed that it might just beat itself out of your chest? Such feelings are usually hard to ignore. And that's because they aren't just feelings; they're important signals through which the body is trying to communicate with you.

Surely, it might be a medical problem. And while your body is communicating with you in that case as well, sometimes it's a warning sign against something different. Something more insidious. Something you never could have guessed on your own.

It might be a sign that you're not in sync with your body's natural rhythm.

But what does it mean to be *in rhythm* in the first place?

Being in rhythm means we're in the most balanced state that our body can be in. It's a form of being that makes us feel happy, safe and sound. It's a state which brings out the best in a person.

But the reverse is also true.

When you're not in sync with your natural rhythm, you may start to feel irritable, anxious and depleted. Nothing seems to work, no matter how hard you try to give your best.

Rhythm is critical for a sound mind and healthy body. It's why we rock a baby when they're crying - to help them find their natural rhythm and calm down. It's also why both children and adults like to engage in different activities to relax themselves and be *in-the-zone*. Some like knitting, some prefer walking while others simply go for a few hours of me-time in order to *tune back in*.

Rhythm is regulating. And we feel regulated when we're in balance.

The natural balance in our body is maintained by different biological systems that are continuously monitoring everything that's going on inside and outside the body. These systems keep a keen eye for any sign that our safety and wellbeing is threatened. For instance, they make sure that we have enough food, water and oxygen at all times and give clear indications when our precious balance is in jeopardy.

Remember that sudden fluttering of the heart we talked about earlier? That is just one of those warning signs.

But being in balance isn't just about meeting bodily needs. It also depends on factors such as the quality of our relationships with family, friends, community and nature.

Right from when a person is an infant, they learn to maintain their balance and regulate themselves. A baby cries because they feel unregulated due to, say, a dirty diaper (It's not just babies that feel unregulated though. Adults might also feel the same). But unlike adults who can fend for themselves and regain balance on their own, a baby depends on their caregivers to regulate them.

And if they're not regulated and brought back into balance by their caregivers, they might lose their ability to regulate themselves as an adult.

Without regulation, there is no balance. And without balance, there is no rhythm.

All life is rhythmic.

From the time that a child is conceived, they receive rhythmic input from their mother's heartbeat. It is from here that the child first begins to develop a sense for what is a well-regulated rhythm (approximately 60-80 beats per minute). Any loss of rhythm, or vibrations that are significantly higher or unpredictable, means there's danger.

Something's not right.

But things change when the caregiver intervenes, more so when they intervene in a loving manner. For instance, they come to feed the crying baby while calming them down.

This cycle keeps itself repeating; the infant feels dysregulated, they cry for attention, the caregiver intervenes in a loving manner. Ultimately, it is these countless moments of loving and attentive care which then combine together to form a rewarding and regulating connection with the caregiver.

But the impact of these rewarding interactions isn't just limited to the caregiver. These loving and warm moments also help the infant develop the ability to connect to other people in healthy relationships. This ability to connect with others, regulate and be regulated, reward and be rewarded, is what ultimately forms the basis of thriving families and communities.

A consistent pattern of attention and love by the caregiver also creates a positive worldview in the mind of a child; that people are safe and can be relied upon. This positive worldview then creates a spiral of goodness and positivity all around; when a person projects positive expectations out into the world, they actually bring out the good in others. This further reinforces their positive mindset and the cycle continues.

But a parent who is overwhelmed, dysregulated and exhausted can't provide consistent care and attention to their children. Such children not only form a negative view of the world, because they grow up learning that people can't be relied upon, but also develop highly sensitized stress-response systems.

A highly sensitized stress-response system develops when someone deals with circumstances involving unpredictable and uncontrollable stress.

There is a set of core regulatory networks (CRNs) in our brains that work together to keep us regulated and balanced against various stressors. When a child is hungry, cold, or afraid and their caregiver fails to respond in a loving and consistent manner, their stress-response system is activated in an inconsistent and prolonged way. If the child keeps facing these challenges, their CRNs adapt to run in a constant *action* mode.

Even when everything is normal and there's no apparent threat in the environment.

A highly sensitized stress-response system is a direct result of enduring unpredictable, extreme and prolonged stress.

But stress is an essential part of life which is why our body has its own mechanisms in place to deal with a threatening or stressful situation; It either readies itself for *fight-or-flight* or prepares to enter into *dissociative* mode. While the former is meant to tackle the challenge head on, the latter relies on *preparing* to get hurt.

Dissociation is a very common adaptive mechanism, particularly among young children. Victims usually learn to disappear into their inner world (where they're safe, free and in-control) as their body begins to brace itself for an oncoming assault.

But regulation never comes easy for those who have suffered from prolonged trauma or abuse. That is because this prolonged exposure to challenging circumstances has altered their stress-response system, sometimes permanently. Regulation, in such cases, may take the form of extreme and destructive measures. These include, but are not limited to, porn addiction, compulsive eating and even drugs and substance abuse.

Through his work with trauma victims, Dr. Perry has found that most drug users had a history of developmental trauma.

This is precisely why healing from addiction is equated to doing deep spiritual work; when an addiction is confronted and worked upon, one is actually healing themselves from the trauma that *led to that addiction in the first place.*

But trauma isn't the only culprit here. Even if someone has experienced no major traumatic event in their life, being exposed to unpredictable stress and the accompanying lack of control can sensitize their CRNs.

It's why children raised in a household with an addicted parent have a higher chance of being addicts themselves. It's that environmental stress, fear, and threat, as well as the absolute lack of control over things, that forces these young minds to regulate themselves with drugs.

The feeling is not just regulating. It's also rewarding for the brain.

Our brain needs rewards. In fact, we all have our own *reward buckets* to fill in each day.

Since the nature of a reward is such that the pleasure obtained isn't very long lasting, the reward bucket gets emptied every day. Therefore, it must be filled-in on a daily basis.

Each of us fills our reward buckets using the reward fillers at our disposal.

But not every day is a good day. And the reward fillers can be both positive and negative.

Which is why when all is well, we usually fill our reward bucket with positive relational fillers such as meaningful interactions with family or engaging in a favorite activity that restores our rhythm. But when that's just not the case, one might resort to negative fillers like consuming alcohol and drugs or eating more sweet/salty/fatty foods to feel better.

We turn to more negative fillers in the absence of positive ones on a bad day. But the availability of a healthy combination of positive fillers ultimately helps decrease the attraction towards unhealthy or destructive fillers. Meaning, if you have a loving and supportive circle of family and friends around you, you're less likely to drink alcohol to feel rewarded.

The bucket must be filled though. The shortage of positive fillers doesn't really change that.

So when all isn't sunshine and rainbows, it is suggested that you fill your reward bucket with *connectedness*. Connectedness is a sense of belonging that originates from positive interactions with friends, family and other acquaintances. It is the highest form of reward recognized by our brain and is a great means to fill your reward bucket with positive fillers.

Particularly when you're inclined to fill it to the brim with hamburgers, tears and marijuana.

In fact, connectedness is such a powerful and rewarding feeling that trying to regulate someone suffering from substance abuse with alienation and isolation seems so besides the point. Keeping the substance abuser isolated is not going to solve the root of the problem.

In order to be able to really help these people, it's vital that we also ask *What Happened to Them* as part of the treatment. Our biggest failure in treating substance abuse often lies in neglecting the underlying reasons that make someone highly vulnerable to abuse in the first place. A trauma-aware approach is therefore highly recommended when treating substance abuse.

Substance abuse is a matter of dysregulation, more than anything. This dysregulation originates from trauma, abuse or adversity. Or even prolonged exposure to high and unpredictable stress.

As humans, it is our natural instinct to continuously strive for regulation and to seek balance. Some do it with drugs. Others take a walk.

But connectedness remains the most potent form of reward and regulation. It is even critical for those who rely on destructive forms of regulation such as substance abuse or drugs.

Without a circle of caring, loving and supportive folks around, it's almost impossible to break out of self-destructive behaviors.

Or, as we'll learn in a later chapter, even survive.

## Lessons

1. As humans, we're continuously seeking balance and regulation.

2. A child raised with consistent love and care grows up to have a positive worldview. They can regulate themselves effectively and have the ability to connect in healthy relationships.

3. A child that isn't raised with consistent love and care turns out to be extremely sensitive. Their brain is constantly on the lookout for threats in their environment, even when everything's perfectly normal.

4. Substance abuse is a matter of failing to regulate ourselves, more than anything.

5. Connectedness is the greatest form of reward.

## Issues To Think About

1. Rhythm and balance

- Question: What do you understand by the terms 'regulation' and 'balance' after reading this chapter?

_____

_____

_____

_____

- Question: What do you consider your favorite activity to get back in rhythm or in-the-zone?

_____

_____

_____

_____

2. Importance of early childhood care

- Question: What was life like when you were a child?

_____

_____

_____

_____

- Question: Are you doing things differently for your own children? Why or why not?

_____

_____

_____

_____

- Question: How important do you think early childhood care is? why?

_____

_____

_____

_____

- Question: How do you think the way you were taken care of as a child has affected your relationships and stress-response as an adult?

_____

_____

_____

_____

3. Substance abuse and dysregulation

- Question: Do you think substance abuse is a matter of dysregulation? Why or why not?

_____

_____

_____

_____

- Question: How is it that you fill your reward bucket on a daily basis? Is it with more positive fillers or more negative ones? Why?

_____

_____

_____

_____

4. Connectedness

- Question: Have you ever felt the impact of connectedness as the highest form of reward? Please explain in as much detail as possible.

_____

_____

_____

_____

- Question: Have you ever felt the impact of a lack of connectedness in your life? Please explain in as much detail as possible.


_____

_____

_____

_____

## Achieving Targets

1. How to find better ways of regulating yourself and filling your reward bucket with more positive fillers?

2. How to take the best possible care of your children in the first 5 years of their life?

3. How to increase connectedness in your life?

## Actionable Movements

1. Think back to the last time you had an emotional meltdown or felt emotionally overwhelmed.

   Complete the following exercises to understand how to regulate your emotions the next time you face an emotionally charged situation.

   - Be honest and a little curious, what do you think triggered an emotional response in that situation? What was happening around you and did it bring up something from the past?


_____

_____

_____
_____
_____

- What were your physical symptoms at the time? Were you hungry? Were you feeling hot?

_____
_____
_____
_____
_____

- What's the story you were telling yourself? What other explanations were possible? If there's a person involved, add 'just like me' at the end of every sentence you're thinking about them. This works wonders to put things in perspective.

_____
_____
_____
_____
_____

- What's something positive that you could have told yourself at the time? Maybe it's thinking that everyone is doing their best and it's not your fault. Positive self-talk at times like these helps mitigate negative emotions.

_____
_____
_____
_____
_____

- How could you have responded more consciously? Switching your responses may result in completely different outcomes. Always remember that you get to choose how you respond.

_____
_____
_____
_____
_____

2. The first five years of a child's life are developmentally crucial.

Included below are 5 key areas that are important during this period. In the empty space following each, write how you'll implement these in your child's life.

- Implementation of Play

_____
_____
_____
_____
_____

- Healthy eating

_____
_____
_____
_____
_____

- Physical activity

_____
_____
_____
_____
_____

- Physical and mental health

_____

_____

_____

_____

_____

- Neighborhood and local community

_____

_____

_____

_____

_____

3. Explore 5 ways to fill your reward bucket with positive fillers.
   - #1

   _____

   _____

   - #2

   _____

   _____

   - #3

   _____

   _____

   - #4

   _____

   _____

   - #5

   _____

   _____

4. Included below are 5 ways to increase connectedness in your life.

   In the blank space following each, write down how you'll implement these in your own life.

   - How can you build Social Capital? Consider ways in which you might bring people from different backgrounds together through a shared interest.

     _____
     _____
     _____

   - How can you focus on what's right with people rather than what's wrong with them?

     _____
     _____
     _____

   - How can you show more empathy, considering other people's point of view?

     _____
     _____
     _____

   - How can you do more family activities every week?

     _____
     _____
     _____

   - How can you find ways to incorporate 'no-phone times' in your routine?

     _____
     _____
     _____

Checklist

1. We're always looking for ways to regulate and reward ourselves. These can be both positive and negative.

2. The first 5 years of a child's life are crucial to their development. It won't be wrong to say that these can make or break their life and personality.

3. Substance abuse can be treated more effectively with connectedness than isolation.

# Chapter Three – How We Were Loved

### Summary

*How we were loved makes all the difference.*

That's because love is the superglue of our relations.

A sense of belonging, to love, and be loved is what forms the core of human experience. It is the capacity to socialize, form groups and love each other (both individually and in communities) that has been the key to our survival and success on this planet.

And this capacity *to love and be loved* first starts developing in the infancy. In fact, it is the foundation of all development that takes place later in life.

But the word *love* has a deeper meaning than what we typically attribute to it. In reality, it is *how your needs were met* and *how you meet the needs of others* that constitutes love.

In other words, love translates itself to the responsive and attentive care one *receives and gives*.

Consider an infant, for example. When they have a need (they're hungry or cold) and the parent arrives to take care of them in a timely and loving manner, they *feel loved*. The warmth of the parent, their loving touch, scent, sight, sounds and actions are what *grow into* the feelings of love for the baby; without them ever knowing the dictionary meaning of the word 'love'.

And just like a child can feel loved, they can also sense when they aren't loved.

It's this perception about being loved (or not) that shapes a developing child's worldview. They think, *'People are good and reliable. When I have a need, it'll be fulfilled'* or *'People can't be relied upon. They always leave when I need them'.*

But the way a child is loved doesn't just help them develop a positive worldview or invoke feelings of *being loved*. Attentive and loving caregiving also helps build a child's ability to love others by organizing and shaping the core neural networks (CRNs) in their brains.

*You can only love if you are loved.*

It is one's early life experiences that help develop and organize these core regulatory networks (CRNs) in the brain. When the CRNs develop and organize normally, they result in healthy development of areas higher up in the brain. But if this development is disrupted for any reason, all the systems that are influenced by the CRNs get adversely affected.

The following three types of disruptions are known to affect CRNs;

1. Disruption before birth. Happens when an expecting mother is under extreme stress or takes drugs or alcohol.
2. Early interactions with the parent. If there is some form of chaos, disruption or aggressiveness in these early interactions, a developmental adversity may arise.
3. Patterns of stress. Prolonged exposure to unpredictable, uncontrollable and extreme patterns of stress can make the stress-response system overly sensitive.

The effect of early life experiences on a developing child's CRNs and brain shows that *how you were loved* can change the whole biology of the brain. This can impact how a child functions for the rest of their lives. It's like building a house. If the foundation isn't laid out properly, the house will have constructional defects.

And these defects show up. Sooner or later.

When a child is raised in a chaotic, unloving and stressful environment, their brain is organized differently.

And that's because the brain is a malleable organ that is shaped based on how it's used. When stimulated by an activity, there are physical changes in the neural networks of the brain to adapt to the new circumstances. So when for example, a person practices playing piano, the neural networks in their brain involved with playing piano change. This is exactly how practice makes one better at any skill in life, whether it be sports, academics or arts.

This marvelous process of the brain adapting to our individual world is known as 'Neuroplasticity'. Neuroplasticity, however, relies on a key principle. That principle is *specificity*.

So if you want to mold a certain part of the brain to achieve anything specific, that particular part of the brain must be activated. In other words, you must actually carry out the activity in order to bring physical changes to the brain. For example, you must practice playing guitar to form neural networks that make you an expert guitarist. Simply watching videos about how to play a guitar won't work. Similarly, you must actually practice playing soccer to ace the game.

And when it comes to love, you must actually *be loved* in order to *love.*

Because if one isn't loved as a child, the networks in their brain don't organize to love and feel loved.

And that's not all. A child raised in a stressful and chaotic environment also develops an overly sensitive stress-response system.

Most of us think that 'stress' is a bad word. But moderate amount of stress and challenge isn't bad. It's what gets our stress-response system to train and build muscle to deal with life. Moderate stress gets the relevant systems activated so we can be kept healthy, safe and sound.

However, what's troubling is the *pattern* of stress activation. If stress occurs in  unpredictable, uncontrollable, prolonged or extreme patterns, the poor stress-response system becomes sensitized. People with sensitized stress-response systems find even the basic challenges of daily life daunting. This ultimately impacts their emotional, behavioral and physical health.

On the contrary, when the pattern of stress in a person's life is fairly predictable, moderate and controllable, their stress-response system becomes *resilien*t. People with a resilient stress-response system have a stronger, more flexible stress-response capability and can better deal with the challenges of life.

And that's a good thing. Because stress is an essential, and often unavoidable, part of life.

When faced with a stressful situation, our body responds in one of the two ways; *arousal* or *dissociation.* Arousal is the *fight or flight* response. It's when our body gets ready for combat. Adrenaline is released. Muscles are supplied with more blood than usual. And the heart rate revs up.

*Dissociation,* on the other hand, is a more laid back approach against an oncoming threat. It involves backing off from the external world and reaching out to our inner world. It turns on the protective mode, instead of the defensive.

Now here's an interesting fact about these two types of responses.

If a stressful situation brings out an *arousal* response in a person, that person will respond with arousal whenever faced with that stressful situation again. So if a child is beaten by their father and she responds with a fight or flight response, any future encounter with her father will always evoke the same response.

If on the other hand, the child is beaten by her father and she responds with dissociation, a future encounter of a similar nature will elicit dissociation.

Different cues in the environment can evoke very different responses by the same person. That's because they might activate memories stored in the lower systems of the brain that can't tell the difference between past, present and future. And with no access to the cortex in a stressful situation, the brain relies on *experience* for an appropriate stress-response.

The point we're getting at here is that our specific trauma-related responses will depend upon the stress response that was dominant in any given experience.

This also indicates that the timing, nature, pattern and intensity of a traumatic experience influences how a person will be impacted.

And if they'll live in fear for the rest of their lives.

Our brain functions in a 'state-dependent' manner.

As we move from one state to another, different parts of the brain get activated.

When there's a threatening situation looming, the control shifts from the higher parts of the brain to the lower parts. This directly impacts functioning as critical thinking is shut down in favor of a more reactive approach to the situation. One starts thinking *in the moment*.

*'State-dependent'* functioning is completely normal and absolutely vital under normal circumstances.

However, prolonged exposure to stress and trauma can make one get stuck in a constant state of fear and terror. This isn't bad, given the challenging situation at the time. But when everything's fine, what was once adaptive becomes *maladaptive*.

And the fact that trauma-related behavior is widely misunderstood in our society makes it even worse.

Which is why it's important for our education, mental health and juvenile justice systems to become more trauma-informed. They shouldn't just look at what a person did or what seems to be wrong with them. Rather they should be asking;

## *What Happened to You?*

### Lessons

1. Children can sense whether they're being loved or not.

2. Given love, the unloved can become loving.

3. A child grows up to be vulnerable or resilient, depending on the quality of early interactions with their caregivers.

4. Our brains are malleable in nature. Prolonged exposure to stress and trauma changes the brain biologically.

5. Stress itself isn't bad. Uncontrollable, unpredictable, prolonged and extreme stress is bad.

6. We need to have a more trauma-aware society and systems.

### Issues To Think About

1. Importance of love

   - Question: Do you feel loved?

     _____
     _____
     _____

   - Question: Did you ever feel that you were unable to experience love and connection with other people? Why?

_____
_____
_____

- Question: What do you think makes a person feel loved? Why?

_____
_____
_____

2. Resilience

- Question: Do you consider yourself a resilient person? Why or why not?

_____
_____
_____

- Question: What kind of childhood did you have? Do you think it provided enough resilience-building opportunities?

_____
_____
_____

3. Fear

- Question: What is your biggest fear in life?

_____
_____
_____
_____

- Question: Do you consider yourself brave?

_____
_____
_____
_____

- Question: Do you think it's possible to overcome fear?

_____
_____
_____
_____

4. Trauma-aware society and systems

- Question: Why do you think we need to have more trauma-informed systems? How can these help those affected by trauma?

_____
_____
_____
_____

- Question: How do you think we can increase awareness about trauma in our society?

_____
_____
_____
_____

## Achieving Targets

1. How to love and feel loved?

2. How can you raise your children to be more resilient?

3. How can we overcome our fears?

4. How can we have a more trauma-aware society and systems?

<u>Actionable Movements</u>

Included below are some psychological issues that can prevent you from falling in love. Find out which of these may apply to you and notice how you feel about them.

| Psychological issue | Does this apply to you? | Describe your feelings |
|---|---|---|
| **Fear of intimacy** - fear of being fully seen for who you are | | |
| **Low self-worth** - feeling that there's something wrong with you so you're not worthy of love | | |
| **Dependency** - believing that you can't take care of yourself on your own | | |
| **Abandonment issues** - constantly feeling that you'll be betrayed and the other person will leave you | | |
| **Codependency** - 'confusing pleasing' others with love then suddenly feeling 'out of love' | | |
| **Attachment issues** - feeling like you can't trust anyone or depending on another person feels manipulative | | |

| | | |
|---|---|---|
| **Childhood abuse** - feeling attracted to the wrong kinds of people, not trusting anyone | | |
| **Addictive behaviors** - related to work, exercise or eating patterns coming in the way of love | | |
| **Perfectionism** - seeking the perfect partner that doesn't seem to exist | | |

1.  Included below are 5 ways to help make your child feel more loved.

    In the blank space following each, write down how you'll implement these in your relationship with your child.

    - Listen to your kid

    _____
    _____
    _____
    _____

    - Plan fun activities together

    _____
    _____
    _____
    _____

    - Go for small gestures

    _____
    _____
    _____
    _____

- Create a special routine together

  _____

  _____

  _____

  _____

- Include them in your family decisions

  _____

  _____

  _____

  _____

2. Included below are 5 ways to help raise your child to be more resilient.

   In the blank space following each, write down how you'll implement these in your child's life.

   - Be intentional with your interventions and decisions. For instance, decide when you'll intervene in helping them complete a difficult school assignment.

     _____

     _____

     _____

     _____

     _____

   - Resist the urge to eliminate all risk, some risk is necessary for building resilience.

     _____

     _____

     _____

     _____

     _____

   - Teach them some problem-solving techniques that they can use in a particular situation.

_____
_____
_____
_____
_____

- Avoid asking 'why' questions. Instead ask more 'how' questions.

_____
_____
_____
_____
_____

- Don't provide all the answers. Promote a problem-solving answer-seeking approach.

_____
_____
_____
_____
_____

3. Included below are 5 ways to help defeat fear.

In the blank space following each, write down how you'll implement these in your life.

- Take time out - distract your mind for a few minutes so you can actually think.

_____
_____
_____
_____
_____

- Breathe through panic and simply feel it. It helps to take the fear of fear away.

_____
_____
_____
_____
_____
_____

- Face your fears. Avoiding them only makes them bigger.

_____
_____
_____
_____
_____

- Imagine the worst case scenario. Then think if it can actually happen.

_____
_____
_____
_____
_____

- Look at facts. Has this ever happened before?

_____
_____
_____
_____
_____

- Talk about it. It takes the scariness away.

_____
_____
_____
_____
_____

## Checklist

1. It's possible to learn how to love and feel loved.

2. Early life experiences have the potential to make a child resilient or vulnerable.

3. You don't have to live in a constant state of fear. You can overcome your fears.

4. We need to have a more trauma-aware society and systems.

# Chapter Four – The Spectrum of Trauma

<u>Summary</u>

*"Trauma is difficult to reconcile"*

*-Oprah Winfrey*

At this point in our conversation, we've talked a lot about how the actions of a caregiver affect a child.

On the flip side, an unloving and unattentive caregiver is also affected by their own caregiver. And so on.

Trauma leaves its impact on generations and across communities. Most people suffering from its effects don't even realize the impact it has had on their lives. It infects marriages, erodes friendships, destroys work relationships and every other social interaction that a person might have. And more often than not, it leads to tragic endings.

But how does someone know they have been affected by trauma? Is there a clinical definition of what constitutes a traumatic event? Does every bad experience that's hard to forget count as trauma?

The answer, unfortunately, isn't quite straightforward.

Although the wreckage left behind by trauma isn't something experts haven't witnessed before, they have been unable to properly define it. That's because there's a lot of subjectivity involved. Everyone has their own definition of what is considered a *'bad'* or *'traumatic'* event. Additionally, what is or isn't a traumatic situation depends on the things going on inside the person experiencing it and how their stress-response systems were activated.

And since the way in which someone internally experiences trauma differs from person to person, its long term impacts vary accordingly.

In other words, different people going through the same traumatic event respond to it, and are affected by it, differently. For some, it is just a resilience-boosting exercise for the stress-response system. For another person in the same situation, it might be a life-changing event that haunts them forever.

Correspondingly, the long term effects of trauma also vary and depend on many factors; how the stress-response system was activated, whether the event brought an arousal or dissociative response, what was the intensity of the event, if the event was repetitive etc.

All that seems fine. Except that it raises an important question; *how can experts study the impact of trauma when there is no standardized definition of what constitutes trauma?*

Good point.

Even better? The experts have an answer!

A group of experts, gathered by the Substance Abuse and Mental Health Services Administration (SAMHSA), suggest the 'three Es' definition of trauma; the event, the experience, the effect.

But even the 3Es definition of trauma isn't guilty of being completely satisfactory either. The reason, again, is subjectivity. Consider the covid-19 pandemic. Even with its devastating effects on our lives and economy, the pandemic can't be considered traumatic for EVERYONE. Each individual experienced it differently. And while it was undoubtedly traumatic for some people, it was merely stressful for others.

So what's the solution?

Dr. Perry believes that trauma can be best understood by studying its impact on the stress-response system rather than considering, for example, the severity of the event. He suggests that sometimes seemingly minor situations - humiliation, shaming or other emotional abuse - can also cause trauma. That's because in some cases (and for some people), these events play a major role in sensitizing the stress-response system.

And therefore result in long-term effects on the brain and body.

The impact of trauma on physical and mental health depends on certain factors, including the age at which it occurred.

Childhood trauma can be more damaging. Statistics show that Adverse Childhood Experiences or ACEs cause 45% of all childhood mental health issues and 30% of those found in adults.

Also, some noteworthy ACE studies have discovered a link between childhood adversity and the nine major causes of death in adults.

But, beware.

This *correlation* mustn't be confused with *causation*.

Having a high ACE score doesn't mean that you're doomed. Many people with a high ACE score fare quite well in life. On the contrary, having a low ACE score doesn't guarantee that life has dealt you a good hand. Many people with an ACE score as low as one find that they couldn't do as well in life.

So while the ACE scores are really important, they can't be relied on to predict one's fate in life. And there are a few reasons for that.

The ACE questionnaire consists of just 10 questions, all of which have a yes/no answer. Each of these questions addresses some form of adversity. However, a paltry list of 10 questions can't be expected to cover every adversity out there.

Secondly, the initial ACE studies were mostly completed by white middle-class folks. So understandably, the results couldn't be extended to a more diversified population.

Moreover, *a number can't be your whole story.*

Another major lacking factor of the ACE scores is that they can't tell about the timing, pattern and intensity of the stress experienced. As you might recall, the pattern of stress is really important to understand someone's personal trauma and how it might affect their life and health.

The ACE score also doesn't take into account the effects of connectedness. Connectedness is measured by the quality of your relationships with friends, family and community. It is said to have a buffering capacity because it can cancel out some of the harmful impacts of trauma on a person. Which is why connectedness is believed to be a better predictor of someone's mental health than their history of trauma.

Or an ACE score, for that matter.

The timing of adversity is crucial to its impact on one's life. Trauma experienced in, say, the first two months of a child's life can have a more profound impact on long term health and development. Such a child usually does worse than a kid the same age but with better early life experiences. Even if placed in a better environment later in life.

All thanks to the timing of the traumatic experience.

Hard times faced earlier in life sensitize the stress-response system. The effects are more pronounced, since a child is in the developing stage of their life. Resultantly, they cultivate physical and mental health problems as well as behavioral issues.

Professional intervention might be a solution. But even that isn't always helpful.


A major reason for failure of intervention measures is that the educators, caregivers and mental health professionals dealing with a child misunderstand the problem. They think, '*What's wrong with them*?' instead of asking '*What might have happened to them*?' Consequently, the child is misdiagnosed with conditions like ADHD while the real problem is never cured. Because it's never addressed in the first place.

Prevention really is the cure here.

The power and potential of early childhood intervention mustn't be underestimated. If a young parent is supported in the early days of parenthood, their child has a better chance of developing a stronger stress-response.

Both '*time*' and '*timing*' are of essence here. The value of any positive intervention increases manifold when the timing is right. Similarly, the ideal time duration for any positive intervention is *brief*.

This is backed by brain science. Our neural networks are more responsive to *moments*.

Small bursts of positive interference also work best because our brain has its own protective mechanism in place against trauma. These mechanisms ensure that one has only seconds to revisit agony from the past before their brain jumps in and starts doing its own thing to prevent further damage. This is precisely why one can't stand revisiting past trauma for longer periods of time.

Also...

Once the stress-response system is sensitized, it can't be brought back to normal in a short amount of time. Slow and controlled doses of therapy are required to calm it down. And while formal therapy is just one way to heal, a bunch of loving and caring people in your surroundings can do just the same.

It's why talking to a good friend feels therapeutic. They tell you what's on their mind, you tell the same. And it is in those long conversations that you both profit from countless brief therapeutic moments.

These interactions provide a short but effective dose of rewarding, regulating and bonding experiences. They reassure you that you aren't losing your mind and that what you're feeling is completely reasonable given the circumstances.

That is the essence of a therapeutic experience.

To feel *seen* and *heard* after you've suffered from trauma.

Trauma experienced at any age can also cause a host of symptoms known as Post-Traumatic Stress Disorder (PTSD). These symptoms ensue are divided into four clusters; Someone diagnosed with PTSD has symptoms from each of these four clusters.

The 4 symptom clusters are;

- **Intrusive** - symptoms in the intrusive cluster include dreams or nightmares about the event as well images and thoughts that one can't seem to shake away. As trauma shatters our existing worldview, revisiting the event in the form of dreams or thoughts is our brain's way to create a new reality. Intrusive symptoms are, therefore, part of the healing process.

- **Avoidant** - avoidant symptoms arise when facing a person, place, or scenario that brings up painful memories. It is part of a protective mechanism to deliberately avoid any cues that remind of a traumatic event. Early childhood trauma experienced in relation to intimate relationships (say, parents), brings out an avoidant response even when there's no evocative cue present. Childhood abuse within the context of close relationships therefore poisons intimacy - both emotional and physical.

- **Depressive** - these include sadness, a constant sense of guilt, loss of interest and pleasure from anything and emotional as well as physical exhaustion. Broadly speaking, these symptoms consist of changes in the mood and thinking of a person that are often uncontrolled.

- **Hyperarousal** - symptoms in this cluster include hypervigilance, anxiety, sleep difficulties, variable heart rate and irritability. These symptoms arise due to an extremely reactive and high-strung stress-response system.

Even with these broad symptom clusters, trauma doesn't always materialize in the form of PTSD. It can also cause depression, anxiety and other physical as well as mental health problems.

But no matter how trauma presents itself in a person's life, to understand its effects one must ask;

## What Happened to you?

### Lessons

1. What constitutes trauma is different for everyone.

2. Formal therapy can only go so far. A supportive circle of friends and family can do just the same or might even do much more.

3. Short and brief 'bursts' of positive interventions are more effective than long therapeutic sessions.

4. The effects of trauma don't always manifest in the form of PTSD. In fact, trauma doesn't exhibit itself as PTSD most of the time.

# Issues To Think About

1.  Trauma and its effects on mental and physical health

    - Question: Do you think the COVID-19 pandemic is traumatic for you? Why or why not?

      _____

      _____

      _____

      _____

      _____

    - Question: Keeping in mind the 3Es definition of trauma, can you recall a past event that might have traumatized you?

    - Event (what happened?):

      _____

      _____

      _____

      _____

      _____

    - Experience (how did you feel?):

      _____

      _____

      _____

      _____

      _____

    - Effect (how do you think it affected you?):

      _____

      _____

      _____

      _____

      _____

- Question: Have you ever felt the effects of trauma on your physical and/or mental health? Please explain in as much detail as possible?

_____

_____

_____

_____

_____

- Question: Have you ever found talking to a good friend therapeutic? Why or why not?

_____

_____

_____

_____

_____

- Question: Do you think professional therapy is absolutely necessary for treating the effects of trauma? Why or why not?

_____

_____

_____

_____

_____

2. Adverse Childhood Experiences (ACEs).

- Question: As a new mother or father (even if you've given birth one, two, three times), how secure, taken care of and understood did you feel? How do you think the situation would have changed if you had some form of support?

_____

_____

_____

_____
_____

- Question: Do you think young children are more affected by trauma? Why?

_____
_____
_____
_____
_____

- Question: Have you ever taken the ACE quiz? If so, how accurately do you think your score explains the current trajectory of your life?

_____
_____
_____
_____
_____

## Achieving Targets

1. How can you explore and resolve issues related to trauma and its long term impact on physical and mental health?

2. How can you develop healthy cognitive patterns, beliefs and skills about self and increase self-esteem?

3. How can you replace self-defeating beliefs and behavior patterns with self-affirming beliefs and behavior patterns?

4. How can you reduce the negative impact of past trauma (physical and emotional) and move towards healthy relationships?

# Actionable Movements

1. Write down your 3 biggest takeaways from this chapter

   - #1

     _____

     _____

     _____

   - #2

     _____

     _____

     _____

   - #3

     _____

     _____

     _____

2. Included below are some cognitive restructuring techniques that can help you notice and change destructive thought patterns and increase self-esteem.

   In the black space following each, write down how you'll implement these in your own life.

   - How can you monitor and notice your thoughts? What are they? When and where do they come up?

     _____

     _____

     _____

     _____

     _____

   - How can you question your thoughts and assumptions? Are they based on facts? Are they accurate? Are they exaggerating the situation?

_____

_____

_____

_____

_____

- How can you gather evidence that either supports or counters your thoughts and assumptions?

  _____

  _____

  _____

  _____

  _____

- How can you conduct a cost/benefit analysis? How can you compare the cost of your feelings to their benefits in order to understand how damaging they are?

  _____

  _____

  _____

  _____

  _____

- How can you create a more rational, factual and positive explanation of an event or situation to replace your negative thoughts?

  _____

  _____

  _____

  _____

  _____

3. Included below are 10 simple ways to reduce the effects of everyday stressors on your mind and body.

In the blank space following each, write down how you'll implement these in your life.

- Get more physical activity

  _____

  _____

- Follow a healthy diet

  _____

  _____

- Minimize phone use and screen time

  _____

  _____

- Consider taking supplements

  _____

  _____

- Set time aside to practice self-care

  _____

  _____

- Reduce caffeine intake

  _____

  _____

- Spend quality time with friends and family

  _____

  _____

- Avoid procrastination. Stay on top of your priorities

  _____

  _____

- Do yoga or meditation

_____

_____

- Spend more time in nature

_____

_____

4. Think back to the last time you faced a trauma reminder/memory/cue. Complete the following exercise to understand how to deal with it the next time you face it.

   - Step #1: Relax. Breathe in and think 'Let'. Breathe out and think 'Go'.

   - Step #2: Figure out what the reminder/cue/trigger was. Was it a thought, memory, conversation, situation, or place? Be as candid as possible.

   _____

   _____

   _____

   _____

   _____

   - Step #3: Remind yourself that this is just a reminder/trigger/memory and that the trauma isn't happening again.

   - In the space below, describe how you were in a different situation back then than your traumatic experience.

   _____

   _____

   _____

   _____

   _____

5. Make a list of specialists or support groups for PTSD.
   - Person/Group 1—

   _____

- Person/Group 2—

_____

- Person/Group 3—

_____

- Person/Group 4—

_____

- Person/Group 5—

_____

## Checklist

1. What constitutes trauma is different for everyone.

2. Most people don't even realize the effects trauma has had on their lives.

3. The ideal dose of therapy isn't hours long. .

4. A majority of people suffering from trauma _don't_ have PTSD.

5. Your ACE score isn't a crystal ball. It can't predict your future with as much accuracy as you might think.

6. _'What Happened to You?'_ is always a better question to ask than _'What's Wrong With You?'_

# Chapter Five – Connecting The Dots

## Summary

Connecting the dots between *What Happened to You* and how it might affect you is the key.

Key to understanding why you're feeling what you're feeling.

And, more importantly, why you react to things the way you do.

It is important to regain control and stop yourself from falling back into the deepest darkest pit of your worst fears.

Fears that might be uniquely yours. Or inherited from generations before. And in case you're wondering, it's quite possible for a heightened sense of fear to be inherited.

The fear of the grandparent becomes the fear of the parent and then the child. The child then grows up to pass it on to future generations. And so on. Which makes *What happened to us* and those before us, and even those before them, relevant to our discussion.

What we inherit from previous generations impacts us in complicated ways. There's a part played by everything, from genetics to family to community to society and culture. It was the fear of dogs, transmitted through generations, that was used against black folks in the civil rights movement. Just as it was used decades before in the era of slavery to hunt, track and attack black bodies.

Remember, a heightened sense of fear can be inherited.

Like fear, there are other psychological traits, emotional characteristics and behavior patterns that can also be inherited. These are passed down from one generation to the next over long stretches of time through something known as transgenerational transmission.

Transgenerational transmission can take place in many forms. Some characteristics and traits are transmitted through genes, others through epigenetic factors, and even others through postnatal or perinatal experiences such as language, values and beliefs.

But even if we have no control over what we inherit, it doesn't mean that everything is lost.

Dr. Perry believes that a better understanding of how we get our emotional, psychological and behavioral heritage can help us deal with it. And even overcome some of its negative aspects.

And it all boils down to *transmissibility*.

While certain abilities such as associating sound with image are genetic, there are others that are more experience-based. Think about language. Although there are no genes for the Spanish language, children born in a Spanish household grow up to speak the language fluently. That's because language is a *transmissible* skill.

When a baby is spoken to in a certain language, their sponge-like brain changes to learn it, recognizing it as family language. This experience-dependent phenomenon is not just limited to language but also applies to values and beliefs. We learn these as they're passed down from generation to generation through experience.

This ability to transmit skills, beliefs and values to future generations is uniquely human.

We have the ability to take what we've learnt from previous generations, make it better through invention, and pass it on to the future generations. All thanks to our brain, specifically, the cortex. In fact, a lot of human experiences are invented and not genetic.

But what if we inherit generations of negative experiences? How can one deal with that?

Fortunately, it's possible to disrupt the transgenerational transmission of negative experiences and replace them with positive ones. It begins with understanding how each and every aspect of our world impacts us in powerful and often unnoticeable ways.

Whether we're aware of it or not, our surroundings are filled with bias. Superiority, dominance and hatred is emanant in our words and actions. And it's all taken up by our brain, specifically the young developing brains that are absorbing all they can from their environment.

As we discussed earlier as well, the cortex is extremely malleable. It's shaped by the skills we learn, the beliefs we absorb and the values we internalize.

For someone inheriting generations of negative experiences, beliefs and values, this might seem like bad news.

But the very flexible nature of the cortex also means that it can be shaped by both positive and negative experiences. Ultimately, it's this unique *adjustability* of the cortex and the brain that makes it possible to reverse the damage.

If we want to transmit more positive beliefs, values and experiences to our future generations, we must be extremely mindful of the environment they're exposed to. We also need to be super intentional about our words, actions and anything else that might influence our young.

Because *each and everything matters*. Whether it has happened to us, our parents, or to our forefathers. It is the collective accumulation of these decades of experiences, good and bad, that eventually shapes our thoughts, actions, feelings and behaviors.

And one of the most important ways this information is transmitted among generations is through 'genes'. Let's take an example. Do you know that some aspects of our stress-response system are inherited? This is what allows some folks to have an exceptional capacity to endure difficulties while others seem to be highly sensitive to adversity.

It's really *in their genes*!

Just like those genes related to the stress-response system, some *'Epigenetic'* factors are also inherited.


Each cell in our body has the same genes, but not all of them are activated at the same time. Under normal circumstances, there's no need for that. The cells in your brain don't need the genes related to bones or blood. So these are 'turned off' in brain cells and vice versa.

But in emergency situations such as extremely low blood sugar levels, the body calls these idle genes out. It therefore activates them to help with survival. This 'activation' process involves initiating some epigenetic protocols. Resultantly, some surface level changes are made in those 'switched off' genes.

This is done in an effort to keep our body regulated and balanced.

Because as you might remember, *regulation* is vital.

These epigenetic changes can alter the stress-response system, either sensitizing it or making it more resilient. Sometimes, they are stored in the egg or sperm and transmitted to future generations. But the future generations may find no use for them as they're in a completely different situation. So they don't need these epigenetic changes to lead a good and balanced life. Consequently, once adaptive changes become maladaptive.

Luckily, our brain remains flexible to change. This means that the epigenetic changes that regulate genes can be reversed for good.

Just like the impact of emotional and behavior patterns inherited from our ancestors can be reversed.

But how?

The answer lies in *connecting* the dots. Because the past remains a part of our lives.

And it's only once someone has had the opportunity to explore what happened to them, and those before them, that they can understand how it impacts them and how this impact can be reversed.

But connecting the dots from one's past with their current state of affairs isn't always easy.

One reason is developmental trauma. Childhood adversity can have lifelong impact on a person's life. Regardless of what emotional and behavior patterns and experiences and beliefs are passed down from previous generations.

Developmental trauma can harm one's *'attachment'* capabilities. This can show up as relationship troubles with friends, family, partners and co-workers.

Developmental trauma can also cause all kinds of physical health issues. Diabetes is a great example. Trauma alters the core regulatory networks (CRNs) that can cause widespread regulatory problems. This includes the regulation of blood sugar and insulin release. Those with a history of adversity are not only at a high risk for developing diabetes, they also have a hard time managing the disease.

Which makes diabetes more than just a biological condition.

It's the same with abdominal pain and headaches. These trauma-related physical symptoms are often dismissed as *'it's all in your head'*. But they're a common occurrence among people with a sensitized stress-response system.

As we dig deeper into how our brain works, it becomes clear that a change in the brain leads to a change in the physical body. There's no mystery in how talking to a good friend leads to better functioning of the heart and lungs or how a person's 'worldview' impacts their immune system.

There's only neuroscience. And the marvelous connection between our physical and emotional well being. Which, unfortunately, remains widely misunderstood.

Doctors frequently label symptoms such as headaches, abdominal pain and seizure-like episodes as *'psychological'*. They routinely dismiss any chance of a link between these physical symptoms and a history of trauma. When, in fact, understanding the connection between one's physical and emotional health is critical to appreciate *What Happened to them* and how it affects them.

And then there's miscommunication in our brain that impacts our perception of reality. This can also cause further complications in the process of connecting the dots of your past to your current state of affairs.

You might remember that our brain not only develops from the bottom up, but it also processes information in a similar *sequence*. Understanding this *'sequential'* ability of the brain is very important to appreciate why we may see things differently from what they actually are.

The problem with this sequential processing of information is that the lower parts of the brain can't *'tell time'*. They're unable to differentiate between two similar events that happened decades apart. But before the upper more sophisticated parts of the brain have a chance to intervene, the lower primitive parts have already made their call. And that's often a 'miscommunicated' and 'misunderstood' call owing to the very nature of how the lower parts of our brains work.

Now guess who is to be blamed for miscommunication within the brains of two people?

Whenever you're reasoning with someone, you must get to their cortex in order to get your point across and have a meaningful back and forth. But that's not an easy job. Due to the natural sequencing in our brains, your argument has to go through the lower parts before it can reach the higher, more *'intelligent'* sections. Now imagine if the other person is angry, fearful or frustrated.

There's no way you can access their cortex because it's shut down.

So there's no adult conversation for you two at least.

On the contrary, if that person is calm and well-regulated, then you can establish a safe connection right up to their cortex. This allows for more effective reasoning and makes it possible for an *adult conversation* to happen.

But that's usually not the case when there's an actual need for such a conversation.

We've already discussed how fear shuts down the cortex. This implies that if someone isn't feeling safe or is generally frustrated and stressed, it isn't possible to reason with them effectively. One way to eliminate fear is to send signals of familiarity and acceptability. The more positive interactions you have with someone, the more their brain recognizes you as safe and familiar. And the more you have access to the higher, more intelligent parts of the brain to actually have a meaningful conversation.

Another factor that blocks reasoning, particularly between individuals with a greater age difference, is the power differential that naturally exists among them. The brain of a child instinctively perceives the adult as overpowering and bans access to the cortex. The adult therefore has to do more work to decrease this differential and open the roads to communication. One way to do this is by portraying as if they're the same age as the child.

It's only regulation and connection that can open up the doors to effective communication and reasoning.

Just like *connecting the dots* to your past with the present can open the doors of understanding as to why you are the way you are.

But...

Even if we understand *What Happened to Us* and how it impacts us, can we heal from it?

## Lessons

1. We inherit more than just genes from the generations before us. Our ancestors pass on their fears, pain, beliefs and values down to us. Fortunately, we can be the generation that breaks this cycle of negative transmissions.

2. *Each and everything matters.* Whether it has happened to us, our parents, or to our forefathers.

3. Some people really have resilience in their genes!

4. It's only once you've connected the dots between what happened to you, and those before you, that you can understand how it impacts you and how to reverse this impact.

5. Your physical and emotional health are deeply connected. What's happening in your brain affects your body in marvelous ways.

6. Miscommunication between people is actually miscommunication between their brains.

7. It's usually hard to communicate with children because their brains naturally 'block' adults out. Adults may have to act like they're the same age as kids to pass this mental barrier.

## Issues To Think About

1. Racism, bias and discriminative policy making

   • Question: How much do you know about the fears, pain, beliefs and values held by your ancestors?

   _____

   _____

   _____

   _____

   • Question: How do you think your community is affected by the deep-rooted fear, pain, beliefs and values passed down from previous generations? Do you think it's possible to overcome them?

   _____

   _____

   _____

   _____

   • Question: Do you know of any destructive and discriminatory policies against your community that embed racism? What do you think needs to be changed?

   _____

   _____

_____

_____

- Question: Can you point out some of the hidden biases, hatred and hints of superiority in your environment? How do you think these might affect the young minds around you?

_____

_____

_____

_____

- Question: What is your view on the Black Lives Matter movement of 2020?

_____

_____

_____

2. Neglecting the mind/body connection

- Question: Do you or someone you know is affected by a physical health condition? How will you connect it to yours (or their) emotional health?

_____

_____

_____

_____

- Question: Have you ever felt the impact of positive thoughts/emotions/worldview on your physical health? How were you able to make the connection?

_____

_____

_____

_____

3. Effective communication

- Question: Why do you think you have difficulty communicating with certain people? Why do you think there are others you can communicate well with?

  _____
  _____
  _____
  _____

- Question: Have you ever found it hard to communicate with children? How did you overcome this? Why or why not?

  _____
  _____
  _____
  _____

## Achieving Targets

1. How to identify and overcome fear, bias and other negative tendencies and behavior patterns that you might have inherited?

2. How can you be more mindful about your emotional health so you can have better physical health?

3. How can you work on improving your communication skills, particularly with young children?

## Actionable Movements

1. Write down your 3 biggest takeaways from this chapter

- #1

  _____
  _____
  _____

- #2

  _____
  _____
  _____

- #3

  _____
  _____
  _____

2. What is your worst fear? (example: fear of flying)

   _____
   _____
   _____

   Included below are 3 ways to help you overcome your fear above.

   In the blank space following each, write down how you'll implement these in your own life to help overcome your worst fears.

   - How will you face your fears? How can you expose yourself to your fears in a way that might help you overcome it?

     _____
     _____
     _____
     _____
     _____

   - How can you learn more about your fears? How can you keep a record of when it happens, what happens and what helps in managing it effectively?

     _____
     _____

_____

_____

_____

- How can you implement healthy eating habits in your life to help with your fears? (Think: How can I reduce my caffeine and sugar intake?)

_____

_____

_____

_____

_____

3. Find out a discriminatory law or policy that's affecting your community? How do you think your community is being affected?

_____

_____

_____

_____

_____

4. Included below are 4 strategies to help address unconscious bias.

In the blank space following each, write down how you'll implement these in your own life to help discover and uproot your hidden biases.

- How can you increase self-awareness to recognize your biases? How can you monitor your first impressions and reactions to people? Particularly concerning those you don't like or who 'look' different than you.

_____

_____

_____

_____

- How can you widen your social circle to build cultural competence and learn more about others?

_____

_____

_____

_____

- How can you remove bias from any decision you make in the workplace or generally in life?

_____

_____

_____

_____

- How can you make yourself accountable for when you act in a biased manner? How can you be more honest about your biases?

_____

_____

_____

_____

5. Included below are 5 ways to maintain good emotional health.

   In the blank space following each, write down how you'll implement these in your own life to improve your emotional, and in turn, physical health.

   - How can you express your feelings, particularly those related to anger, sadness or frustration in an appropriate way?

   _____

   _____

   _____

_____

_____

- How can you pause yourself and 'think' before you act?

_____

_____

_____

_____

_____

- How can you manage your stress levels?

_____

_____

_____

_____

_____

- How can you connect with others in more positive ways?

_____

_____

_____

_____

_____

- How can you have a more positive outlook on life?

_____

_____

_____

_____

_____

6. How will you reason with someone who is fearful, angry or frustrated?

Start with step #1 below. Fill each step out with what you think might work for effective communication with such a person.

- Step #1: Regulate (Think: Will they respond better when calmed down? What can you do to achieve that?)

  _____
  _____
  _____

- Step #2: Relate/connect (Think: How can I have more positive interactions with them?)

  _____
  _____
  _____

- Step #3: Reason (Think: How will I reason with them so they don't feel like I'm simply blaming them?)

  _____
  _____
  _____

## Checklist

1. We inherit both good and bad stuff from our ancestors.

2. Our physical and emotional health are deeply connected.

3. In order to reason well with someone, make sure they're calm and in a state to understand what you're saying.

4. The past of the generations before us still lives inside us.

# Chapter Six – From Coping To Healing

<u>Summary</u>

*"Neglect is as toxic as trauma"*

*-Dr. Perry*

Dr. Perry once treated two children with the same diagnosis; ADHD, major depression, intermittent explosive disorder and conduct disorder.

But there were some strange differences between them.

Despite being diagnosed with the same conditions, both children showed behaviors that were poles apart. They also responded very differently to treatment. According to Dr. Perry, these differences came from *What Happened to Them* as children.

One of these children, Thomas, had a good early start. His father wasn't always abusive. It was only after the father returned from Vietnam and had PTSD that he became violent. But Thomas was lucky in that his mother and other family members at least tried to protect him from his father's brutal beatings.

This provided a buffering or protecting effect.

Together with his relatively better start in life and this buffering effect, Thomas developed healthy relational neurobiology and responded well to treatment.

James, on the other hand, was an entirely different case. It seemed as if no amount of therapy could heal him. But then, he came from a very different background than Thomas.

James was abandoned by his mother when he was just 3 months old. After spending six weeks in shelter care, a very weary grandmother took him in. But she wasn't happy with her decision to adopt James at all. Consequently, James turned out to be extremely disobedient and inattentive. His behavior sprung from many things; his mother's disappearance when he needed her the most,

72

being cared for at the shelter by one stranger after another and the grandmother's disengaged and bitter upbringing.

Both stories, although contrasting, hold an important lesson.

When looking at *What Happened to You*, it's important to also look at *What Didn't Happen for you*?

It was the things that didn't happen for James that made all the difference; lack of love and attention as well as absence of a nurturing touch and reassurance that every child needs.

In other words, James was *neglected*.

It's not uncommon to see neglect and trauma occur side by side. However, both of them cause different biological experiences and affect the developing brain very differently.

So, what exactly is neglect?

When a child is in the developing stage, they need some essential stimulation and experiences to express their genetic potential. Neglect can be detrimental at this stage. That's because it interferes with the timing, pattern and nature of these important experiences that the child absolutely needs for their development.

Early neglect can cause under-development of key capabilities such as walking, talking and even forming relationships. Children raised in neglectful environments fail at simple tasks such as using utensils or going to the toilet. All because the key neural networks in their brains do not receive the right experiences at the right times. So these children grow up with many deficits.

The longer a child spends in a neglectful environment, the harder it will be for them to recover from it.

During the first six years of a child's life, there are many important things happening in their developing brain. Neglect in these early years of life, therefore, is more harmful than that experienced later in life.

There are different forms of neglect, the most common of which is *'fragmented neglect'* Fragmented neglect is just that, fragmented. It has no pattern; some days the caregiver comes to soothe the baby when they cry, other days they don't. And on still other days, they respond with anger or violence.

And since the infant needs a consistent and patterned response to send clear signals to the developing brain, they feel neglected.

Another form of neglect is *'splinter neglect'*. This kind of neglect occurs when some experiences received by the infant are timely and patterned, but others are not. This can lead to normal development in some areas, while others remain ignored or understimulated.

*'Outsourced parenting'* among wealthy parents is yet another form of neglect towards a child. Parents who hire different people to take care of their developing kids don't realize that children need relational consistency early in life. Although it's true that the more attentive and loving people in your life the better, a developing child requires adequate consistency in their early relationships to develop key systems.

For example...

Let's say that an infant is being spoken to in English for 4 weeks and then Spanish for another 4 weeks. And since the parent wants them to learn as many languages as they could, they spend another 4 weeks talking to them in French.

Which language do you think the infant will grow up to be fluent in?

You guessed it right, none.

Even though every language does activate the speech and language part of the brain, there isn't enough repetition with one language to organize the child's full language capability.

Relationships are the same. If a young child's caregiver changes repeatedly and frequently, they can't have the infrastructure to develop healthy relational neurobiology. This is why it is recommended that a child have a few safe, stable and nurturing relationships in their first year of life. This provides enough repetition for them to develop a sound relational architecture that can lead to having many healthy relationships down the road.

A serious problem of today's modern world is that parents are distracted by their phones and laptops when their children need them to be fully present. This is like outsourcing parenthood to gadgets. The young developing brain gets a constant message that the parent is unavailable, leading them to think I'm not important enough. This creates a negative worldview for the child and impacts their capacity to love. They grow up with an insatiable hunger for love that doesn't seem to be fulfilled by anything.

*You can't love if you haven't been loved.*

For an infant whose needs aren't met, the natural fight-or-flight response is to cry. But if that doesn't elicit a loving and caring response by the caregiver, the infant resorts to dissociation. They retreat to their inner world and use dissociation to deal with the pain of unmet needs.

But dissociation isn't just used by a distressed infant as a coping mechanism. Partial dissociation is used by all of us in our daily lives. There are moments when we retreat from the high-pressure world around us to think and act in ways that will be beneficial to us. We still have access to our thinking brain i.e. the cortex, but we disengage from some aspects of our environment to get 'in the zone'.

That's mind-wandering. And it's critical to reflective thinking and creativity.

Dissociation therefore is a great coping mechanism that can help a person deal with challenging everyday situations.

But frequent dissociation can also turn into a *dissociative* disorder.

Dissociative disorder occurs when a person increasingly takes themselves into their inner world. To understand why, let's backtrack a little.

We've already discussed that prolonged, uncontrollable and unpredictable patterns of stress sensitize the stress-response system. It becomes overly active and reactive. And if such a person has dissociation as their primary tool for adapting to stress, then they will dissociate whenever a challenging situation arises. No matter how big or small.

Dissociative disorder can make people sabotage relationships as they try to emotionally disconnect themselves from their partners. Another common behavior in people with a sensitized dissociative response is to cut themselves.

But doesn't that hurt?

Sadly, no. That's because dissociation releases the body's natural painkillers. And for someone with a highly reactive stress-response system, the amount of painkillers released can be massive. This not only makes cutting painless, it feels soothing and regulating. Other maladaptive forms of self-regulation include banging the head on the walls, throwing up or pulling out eyebrows.

But a dissociative disorder doesn't always show up in extreme behaviors. Sometimes, it can develop into personality characteristics that are hard to spot. These characteristics become coping mechanisms for people with a history of adversity.

One such coping mechanism is compliance. Compliance can show up as a tendency to please people at all costs, because one just can't stand to be in a conflicting situation.

But as we've discussed a few paragraphs back as well, not all kinds of dissociative behaviors are bad or harmful. In fact, the ability to control one's dissociative capabilities can be extremely empowering. It allows you to disconnect when you need it the most and make a comeback to deal with the challenge at hand.

It's even possible to eliminate negative forms of dissociative behaviors such as undue compliance using the power of 'intention'.

Think of it this way. An intention goes ahead of everything you think, do or say. Whereas the outcome of your experience depends on the intention you have going into it. So if you start questioning yourself before anything you do and say, *'What is my intention in doing this?'*, it can turn things around for the better.

But even with the power of intention at our disposal, we sometimes make the wrong choices in life. For example, it is very common for victims of trauma to fall into abusive relationships. The main reason for this is that we naturally gravitate towards what' s familiar. This tendency is so strong that people with a history of trauma deliberately sabotage relationships when they find someone who isn't abusive.

Just so they can transport themselves back to the once familiar environment of trauma, abuse and neglect.

Thankfully, it's possible to fix this dilemma.

It requires patience, intentional change and sometimes therapy.

Patience and understanding to help such people have enough new experiences to form a new and improved world view. Intentional change with an understanding of how to connect the dots between everything that happens in your life. And therapeutic help with a view that therapy can't eliminate the past. All it can do is create a better route to lead a good life.

## Lessons

1. Neglect is as toxic as trauma. It's particularly damaging when it happens during the first six years of a child's life.

2. The longer a child spends in a neglectful environment, the harder it will be for them to recover from it.

3. It's important for children to have only a few safe and loving relationships in their first year of life.

4. Daydreaming is not bad. It's a healthy form of dissociation that's important for creative thinking.

5. Patience and intentional change can help reverse the negative behaviors one might have developed due to a history of adversity.

## Issues To Think About

1. Child neglect

- Question: Do you or someone you know was neglected as a child? How do you think it affected you (or them) later in life?

    _____

    _____

    _____

    _____

    _____

- Question: Can you point out a form of child neglect happening in your surroundings? How do you think it's neglectful?

_____
_____
_____
_____
_____

- Question: How do you think the following forms of neglect might play out in real life?

- Physical neglect

_____
_____
_____

- Emotional neglect

_____
_____
_____

- Educational neglect

_____
_____
_____

- Medical neglect

_____
_____
_____

2. Dissociative disorders

Cutting and self-harming

- Question: Did you ever cut or harm yourself in any way? Not as a suicide attempt but just to feel good. Did you actually feel good afterwards?

_____
_____
_____
_____
_____
_____

- Question: Why do you think people cut or harm themselves?

_____
_____
_____
_____
_____

Self-sabotaging relationships and undue compliance

- Question: Have you ever found yourself sabotaging a relationship? Do you recall why you did it?

_____
_____
_____
_____
_____

- Question: How easy do you think it is for you to say 'no'? How often do you say 'yes' when you actually want to say 'no'?

_____
_____
_____
_____
_____

3. Importance of downtime

- Question: What are your views about daydreaming? Do you think it can actually help you achieve your goals? Why or why not?

  _____
  _____
  _____
  _____
  _____

- Question: Have you ever used dissociation as part of a coping mechanism? How did it help you?

  _____
  _____
  _____
  _____
  _____

4. Therapeutic help

- Question: Did you ever get therapeutic help for yourself or someone you know? Do you think it actually helped? Why or why not?

  _____
  _____
  _____
  _____
  _____

## Achieving Targets

1. What can you do to prevent child neglect in your home and community?

2. How can you support creative thinking in the children and adults around you?

3. How can you ensure that you aren't sabotaging any of your relationships?

4. How can you say 'no' more often?

5. How can you learn more about what therapeutic help can or can't do?

Actionable Movements

1. Included below are some ways to help avoid child neglect.

   In the blank space following each, write down how you'll implement these in your own life to make sure that your child isn't being neglected.

   • How can you draw on your family, friends and neighbors to boost support for your family and children?

   _____
   _____
   _____
   _____
   _____

   • How can you share more child responsibility with your partner?

   _____
   _____
   _____
   _____
   _____

   • How can you make sure that your child's environment is free of any potential hazards?

   _____
   _____
   _____
   _____
   _____

- How can you obtain community support from places like your local church or community center to create a nurturing home environment for your child?

  _____

  _____

  _____

  _____

  _____

- How can you ensure that your child is surrounded by only a few safe and stable relationships in the first year of their life?

  _____

  _____

  _____

  _____

  _____

2. Included below are 3 ways you can help prevent child neglect and abuse in your surroundings.

   In the blank space following each, write down how you'll implement these in real life.

   - How can you support a friend, relative or family member in raising their kids, particularly those who are single parents?

     _____

     _____

     _____

     _____

     _____

   - How can you help families with low income raise their children?

     _____

     _____

_____
_____
_____

- How can you increase awareness and eliminate misconceptions about raising children in families around you?

_____
_____
_____
_____
_____

3. Think of 3 ways that you can be more present with your children (example: I won't use my phone when I'm with my kids or we'll have some planned family time every weekend)

- #1

_____
_____

- #2

_____
_____

- #3

_____
_____

4. Included below are some grounding techniques that can help you avoid dissociating excessively.

In the blank space following each, write down how you'll implement these in your life.

- How can you find some ways to stay present in the moment?

_____
_____
_____

- How can you engage your sense of smell, sight, touch, hearing, or taste when zoning out?

_____
_____
_____

- How can you use exercise as a tool for physical fitness as well as a grounding technique?

_____
_____
_____

- How can you be more kind to yourself?

_____
_____
_____

- How can you seek professional help?

_____
_____
_____

5. Fill out the table below which includes some warning signs that you might be sabotaging your relationship. Then see how you might fix them.

| Warning signs | Yes, I do it! | No, I've never done this! | How to fix it |
|---|---|---|---|
| You're not addressing the negative emotions you have about your partner | | | Have an honest discussion with your partner about any doubts or fears |
| You're always criticizing your partner | | | Learn more about yourself and your partner's attachment styles. Stick to constructive criticism only |
| You have given up on your sex life | | | Discuss with your partner if you aren't satisfied with your sexual relationship and ask them the same |
| You fail to keep small promises | | | Keep your word when you've given it! |
| You spend your energy on anything but your relationship | | | Give your relationship the time it deserves, particularly if there's something worth mending |

## Checklist

1. A key part of *What Happened to You* is *What Didn't Happen for You.*

2. Neglect is as bad as trauma, particularly during the early years of a child's life.

3. Failing to be present for your children can lead them to have extremely low self-worth.

4. Not all forms of dissociation are bad. Dissociation is harmful when it gets out of hand.

5. Therapy can't erase the past. It can only create new and better ways to venture into the future.

# Chapter Seven – Post Traumatic Wisdom

## <u>Summary</u>

Like the sun with its massive gravitational pull attracting the planets towards it, trauma has a strong pull. It not only sucks the person experiencing it into its powerful grasp, it also claims their family, friends and coworkers found alongside.

Dealing with trauma is hard and exhaustive, even if you aren't a direct victim. It reminds people of their own sense of helplessness. Which is why it's common for friends, relatives, coworkers and communities to protect themselves from the vicious grip of trauma by *looking away*.

This *looking away* can take many forms; Reducing communication, doing fewer check-ins and not engaging in deep conversations with the affected. Instead, people rely on the resilience of the affected individual or community to get over their trauma.

Almost forgetting that trauma never leaves a person the same again.

One of the hardest things to understand about trauma is that nothing and no one can take the pain away. Yes, people can heal. But simply assuming that they'll get over it never helps.

Even worse is believing that children are born resilient. This is nothing but wishful thinking.

Trauma can have a long-lasting impact on anyone experiencing it, whether it's a child or an adult. The biggest fact that supports this idea is the malleability of our brain. The brain is continuously changing as a result of everything we experience, good or bad. Which is why trauma can't just leave a person untouched, regardless of their age.

That isn't to say that both children and adults don't demonstrate resilience in the face of adversity. It simply proves that adversity or trauma never leaves a person unchanged. No matter how resilient they've become as a result.

This is true even if a child (or a grown-up person) shows no apparent 'real life' problems after experiencing trauma. They may seem to function well in everyday life. But the impact of trauma will be there, often fairly visible using brain imaging techniques. For instance, the brain images of children with no abuse show enough differences in the size of some areas when compared to those that have experienced abuse.

But the best indicator of post-traumatic brain changes are usually *'functional'*. A closer look at whether a child is impulsive or inattentive, depressed or anxious, or how well they form and maintain relationships can show a much clearer picture of the impact of trauma on the brain. Even better than the brain images might.

Thankfully, it's possible to build resilience against the impact of trauma. A key aspect of this resilience-building exercise is *connectedness*. We've discussed connectedness before. It is the capacity to connect with supportive, loving and caring people around you. Connectedness has a buffering effect. It acts as a shield that protects against the harmful impacts of trauma on the mind and body.

Another factor that plays an important role in building resilience is our stress-response capabilities. These abilities start developing in childhood, right from when the child is just a newborn. The earliest challenges that stimulate these stress-response systems are hunger, thirst or cold. When these are dealt with just fine, the child begins exploring the world around them. There they meet other 'moderate' stressors that further build their stress-response capabilities.

Then this child grows up to start school, meet new people and face new personal, social and academic challenges. All these stressors, in moderate doses, help build their stress-response capabilities and resilience.

Throughout this journey, the child's relationships play a key part. They provide the care and nurturing support that these little individuals need to overcome challenges. They motivate the child, helping them master key skills, and lead to their healthy development.

But there's a catch here.

These stressors or challenges, however necessary, must be in the *right* dose. This means that a challenge mustn't be too small or big, or too easy or difficult. It must be *just right* for the specific developmental stage of the child. Otherwise, it may have an opposite effect on their development.

And that's the biggest challenge with a traumatized child; to find the right dose of a stressor that will stimulate their stress-response system effectively. A traumatized child already feels unsafe due to the chaos in their life, so it's hard to get them to try something that's out of their comfort zone.

Even if it's a fairly typical challenge that will stimulate healthy development.

A main rule of healthy development is; A sense of safety and stability provides a foundation for healthy growth. When a child doesn't feel safe or they don't have stability in their environment, they don't develop optimally. More often than not, such children grow up to be *dysregulated* individuals that feel threatened at the slightest hint of confrontation.

Because the chaotic and uncontrollable pattern of stress in their lives has sensitized their stress-response systems. It has become overly active and reactive.

One simply can't reason with a *'dysregulated'* person with words. It's usually best to simply be calm in their presence while simultaneously doing something to regulate yourself; Any form of rhythmic or patterned activity would do such as walking, coloring, kicking a ball back and forth etc.

Regulating a dysregulated person also requires that you let them control when and how much they open up to you. This provides moderate, controllable and predictable interaction in their already chaotic life. Remember, a dysregulated person is the best judge of the dose of therapy they require. When they have control over when and how much of this therapy is administered, it creates an ideal healing environment.

An ideal healing environment also consists of a circle of loving, caring and supportive people that can listen to and be present for us. We heal best in a community where we can return to past trauma in controllable and predictable ways. This allows us to ultimately develop resilience.

And this journey from being *sensitized* to *fairly normal* to ultimately *resilient* is what creates post-traumatic wisdom.

Resilience, however, is an ability that has its own ebbs and flow. It is strengthened in the presence of loving, stable and safe relationships in our lives. Whereas the absence of such relationships breaks even the most resilient of people.

You may feel surprised to hear this, but community is even more effective than formal therapy at healing and development.

Take children, for example. There used to be a time when a small multigenerational clan was responsible for bringing up all the children within the family. Each family member provided just the right set of qualities required by a child for healthy development.

No single person was supposed to be everything for every child.

Now compare this to single-parenting in the modern world. A single individual is required to take care of all the emotional, financial, social and physical needs of their children without any help. Caregiving, that was meant to be shared with the community, is now being managed by one individual who's all on their own.

We live in a world that's filled with relational poverty, no matter how fat our bank accounts may be.

A strong connection to community is not only critical for our physical and emotional health, it's also vital for the healthy development of our children.

It's impossible to gain wisdom in life without getting some scars first. But while adversity is important, one cannot develop post-traumatic wisdom without the support of a nurturing community. Being part of a supportive community of friends, family and coworkers is what allows us to regulate ourselves on a daily basis. It makes it possible to blow off steam from the daily stressors in our life and build resilience.

Without this *buffering effect* of a community, our stress becomes magnified and turns into distress.

And distress is what causes sensitizing of the stress-response system, leading to the same physical and emotional consequences as trauma.

## Lessons

1. Trauma never leaves a person unchanged.

2. Resilience isn't an ability that you're born with. It can be developed in the face of trauma.

3.  An impulsive, inattentive and depressed child who has a hard time learning and forming healthy relationships can be showing signs of post-traumatic impact.

4.  A child will develop strong capabilities to deal with stress and trauma when they receive loving, supportive and nurturing early caregiving.

5.  The best way to communicate with a dysregulated person is to control your own nerves around them. They'll ultimately *catch your calm*.

6.  We heal best in community, not in isolation.

7.  Single parents have a tough, almost impossible, job at hand.

### Issues To Think About

1.  Resilience and building it, the right dose of stressors for a developing child. Resilience in the face of trauma

    *   Question: What do you think it means to be resilient? Do you consider yourself resilient?

        _____

        _____

        _____

        _____

        _____

    *   Question: Do you think it's possible to build resilience? How?

        _____

        _____

        _____

        _____

        _____

2.  Importance of community and support against trauma

- Question: Have you ever had friends and family support you during a traumatic event in life? How did it help you?

_____

_____

_____

_____

_____

- Question: Did you ever help a friend or family member cope with trauma? How was the experience for you?

_____

_____

_____

_____

_____

- Question: What do you think are the benefits of a community life?

_____

_____

_____

_____

_____

3. Parenting
Single parenting

- Question: What do you think are the biggest struggles of a single parent? How do you think these affect a child?

_____

_____

_____

_____

_____

4. Trauma-informed parenting

- Question: Which of these myths do you believe in? Select all that apply.
    - "My love should be enough to erase the effects of everything bad that happened before."
    - "My child should be grateful and love me as much as I love him/her."
    - "My child shouldn't feel love or feel loyal to an abusive parent."
    - "It's better to just move on, forget, and not talk about past painful experiences."

- Question: How important do you think it is for parents and caregivers to be loving, encouraging, accepting, appreciating and supportive of their children?

_____

_____

_____

_____

_____

5. Trauma-informed education systems

- Question: What do you think about the following statement; 'Our kids are not broken, our systems are'

_____

_____

_____

_____

_____

6. Communication

- Question: Have you ever come across an individual who had a hard time managing their emotions? How did you deal with them?

_____

_____

_____

_____

_____

## Achieving Targets

1. How can we develop resilience in the face of trauma?

2. How can we provide more supportive and nurturing caregiving for our children so they can grow up to deal with adversity better?

3. How can we be more supportive of the single parents around us?

4. How to feel connected with our community of family, friends, relatives, neighbors etc?

5. How can our education system become more trauma-aware?

6. How can we be more empathic?

## Actionable Movements

1. Included below are 5 ways to develop resilience.

   In the blank space following each, write down how you'll implement these in your own life.

   - How can you practice positive thinking when faced with a challenging situation?

   _____

   _____

   _____

   _____

   - How can you make sure to deliberately choose your response to a challenge?

_____
_____
_____
_____

- How can you build self-confidence and believe more in yourself?

_____
_____
_____
_____

- How can you develop strong relationships all around you to reduce your stress levels and deal better with adversity?

_____
_____
_____
_____

- How can you learn to be more resilient?

_____
_____
_____
_____

2. Think of 3 ways that you can help someone deal with trauma?

- #1

_____
_____
_____

- #2

_____

_____

_____

- #3

_____

_____

_____

3. Complete the following exercise that'll walk you through how to ask for help when you need it.

- Think who may be able to help you? Be resourceful!

_____

_____

_____

- Think how you'll ask them for help? Remember to be courteous.

_____

_____

_____

- Think how you can best explain the kind of help you need? Don't be shy. Be specific.

_____

_____

_____

- Think how you can be more flexible? There's no one way to get help.

_____

_____

_____

- Think how you can show gratitude for their help and support?

_____

_____

_____

4. Included below are a few ways to increase your community life engagement.

   In the blank space following each, write down how you'll implement them in your own life.

   - How can you do some volunteer work in your community?

   _____

   _____

   _____

   - How can you spend more quality time with the friends in your community?

   _____

   _____

   _____

   - How can you join more social groups, faith-based groups or other support groups in your community?

   _____

   _____

   _____

   - How can you create, explore and benefit from virtual/online opportunities for community life engagement?

   _____

   _____

   _____

5. Included below are a few steps you can take to become a more supportive parent.

   In the blank space following each, write down how you'll implement these in your own life as a parent.

   - How can you be more empathic with your child?

     _____

     _____

     _____

   - How can you make yourself open to learning more from your children instead of teaching them all the time?

     _____

     _____

     _____

   - How can you make more time to connect with your children?

     _____

     _____

     _____

   - How can you be a good listener for your children?

     _____

     _____

     _____

6. Included below are some ways for single parents to give and receive support and help to each other.

   In the blank space following each, write down how these apply to you.

- Which of your friends can support you? Friends who are single parents themselves might understand your struggles better.

  _____

  _____

  _____

- Which people from your local child care center, kindergarten, school, local club, religious or support group can help you?

  _____

  _____

  _____

- How can you prompt other parents to connect with you so you can all share your struggles?

  _____

  _____

  _____

- How can you use social media and online support forums to give/take advice and help each other?

  _____

  _____

  _____

## Checklist

1. People aren't born resilient. They need support to deal with trauma.

2. Children are as affected by trauma as an adult.

3. Children who grow up in a nurturing environment develop stronger abilities to deal with adversity.

4. Parenting is hard. Single parenting is harder.

5. We thrive in community. We heal in community. Our children do better in a community.

6. Communicating with a dysregulated person isn't always easy. Use less words and more calm.

7. A traumatized child has special needs. This must be recognized by all, particularly our educational institutions.

# Chapter Eight - Our Brains, Our Biases, Our Systems

### Summary

Where does healing begin?

It begins with the courage to uncover past trauma and expose the raw and bitter truth of our lives.

But this process of unveiling past trauma sometimes feels deceptive. It may seem like we're finding an excuse for the dilemma in our lives. But the reality is that what we're uncovering is an *explanation*, not an *excuse*.

An explanation as to how we're shaped by our environment.

And how, sometimes, we lose our way in life.

Times have changed.

Many people now know about trauma and its impact on all aspects of life. Today, organizations and systems are moving towards a more trauma-informed approach. However, the term 'Trauma-Informed Care' or TIC itself is interpreted differently by different systems.

That's because, like individuals, each system has their own unique worldview. Similarly, they have their own interpretation of what TIC means. The term itself originated back in 2001 and has since been used by various groups with minimal definition or clarity.

The result is that although many TIC-related buzzwords have emerged, they rarely link to any concrete efforts, plans or policy changes. They're just that, buzzwords.

Long story short, despite several efforts to come up with a common definition of TIC, there is none available. There is, however, consistency in some areas of the definition. But not all.

With that out of the way, it's worth noting that progress is still being made.

*Traumatology*, the study of trauma, is very young at the moment. And while everyone may approach TIC in their own unique way, the essence is still there; to approach people with the awareness that *What Happened to Them* is important.

And then take that awareness to 'act accordingly'.

That's the most accurate interpretation of trauma-informed care that there is.

Being truly trauma-informed requires that you look both inside and outside yourself to identify built-in biases. Discrimination based on race, gender and sexual orientation, to name a few, is a fundamental trauma. Such behavior causes uncontrollable and unpredictable patterns of stress that leads to sensitisation of the stress-response system.


*Marginalized people* are *traumatized people.*

And the solutions we have for them are often further retraumatizing rather than being of help.

To get this into perspective, think about a child who's grown up with distress and trauma. This exposure to trauma not only affects the development of their stress-response system but also impacts their ability to have healthy relationships. They'll also have other *developmental disruptions* such as lacking the language skills of a kid their age.

A child like this is set for failure in a typical school environment. That's because the developmental lagging they suffer with is bound to create frustration and communication difficulties.

So they have two solutions; to shut themselves down or blow up.

Seeing these as behavioral problems rather than trauma-related, this child is typically labeled with mental health issues such as ADHD. They often end up being overly medicated, punished, expelled or even arrested.

Ultimately, they up thinking there's actually something wrong with them; that they're lazy, dumb or simply incompetent.

When in reality, they're only suffering from the impact of trauma.

Our brain makes associations based on our earliest memories. We've already discussed how the brain of a developing child is cataloging all experiences and storing them as memories. We've also talked about how all informational input first gets to the lower parts of our brain before reaching the upper more *thinking* parts.

But a traumatized child isn't aware of these brain associations. They may be triggered by the most innocent cues in the classroom and react to them, often in inappropriate ways. It makes sense for them to retaliate because their cortex is shut down and all incoming cues are only processed by the lower parts of their brain.

But the person at the receiving end doesn't know any better either. They may see these reactions as *'unpredictable'* or *'out of the blue'* because they lack the trauma-aware perspective to understand where they're coming from.

Imagine if our schools and teachers were trained to understand childhood adversity and viewed this behavior differently. They'd end up finding meaningful ways to connect with the traumatized child and understand them better. This would ultimately lead to remarkable improvement in academic performance as well as decreases in such outbursts in the first place.

Everyone would win.

Schools that have been using *trauma-informed* programs report some very promising results. They recognize the importance of healing and resilience-building activities such as sports, music and arts. On the other hand, some schools still employ traditional teaching practices in hopes that they will support learning. In reality, these are the worst for engaging the top parts of the brain.

Like schools, mental health service organizations that have no training or experience in trauma do more harm than good. A typical trauma-ignorant treatment causes mislabelling and overmedication. And a typical mental health system is only crisis-focused.

The ideal solution is to recognize that there's no one-size-fits-all approach to learning, or healing, or anything, for that matter. A trauma-aware clinical team uses a variety of tools to help their patients and follows a specific *sequence of engagement*. This is the same sequence that we talked about earlier; regulate, connect, reason.

But what if someone doesn't have the resources to reach out to a professional trauma-aware clinical team or a therapist?

Thankfully, professional help isn't absolutely required for healing.

Yes, therapy is helpful. But without the element of *connectedness*, it isn't that effective. The ideal mix would be to combine both therapy and connectedness to achieve the best possible outcomes.

And our ancestors already knew this.

They recognized the importance of community, connectedness and healing practices that involved repetitive, rhythmic and rewarding experiences. They knew that isolation was toxic and that humans required community and social connection to thrive.

And to heal from trauma.

Speaking of community, sometimes it is our implicit biases that prevent us from connecting with other humans. Particularly if these humans don't look, speak and feel like what we're used to.

The developing brain, as it's trying to make sense of the world around us, makes memories of the smell, sounds and images of *our* people. These memories are stored in the lowest parts of our brain and exist at a very deep unconscious level. This is why implicit bias related to race is so hard to let go; because they're ingrained deep into the brain.

South Africa is a good example of racism as an implicit bias. Being oppressed by the white community for generations, the blacks often associated *whiteness* with fear. They'd dissociate in the face of any *whiteness*; avoid conflict, when confronted, comply.

Similarly, even after the end of aparthied in 1994, the white people felt more comfortable being dominant. Even though many deny having any racial inclinations, there's an implicit bias towards the black community that shows in their behavior.

And that's the tricky part about implicit bias; one's beliefs and values don't always drive their actions. So while a white person may not have racist thoughts about a black person, their actions may tell otherwise. That's because any anti-racist beliefs they have live high up in the more rational parts of the brain. But the lower parts of the brain still contain 'associations' made earlier in life.

These associations are more readily accessible than any anti-racist beliefs residing in the upper parts of the brain.

When the developing brain starts cataloging experiences and forming memories, it's affected by everything happening around. Since a young child is mostly around their parents, everything they do or say impacts the developing brain. A young kid is also influenced by other adults around them as well as the media. And if they rarely interact with a black individual during this time or the developing brain makes a *bad* association concerning blacks in general, they're more likely to cultivate implicit bias as they grow up.

In fact, everybody develops some form of implicit bias based on where and how they grow up.

Implicit bias is one of the main reasons law enforcement absolutely needs trauma training. There will hopefully be less incidents of white cops heedlessly shooting black teenagers, fearing all black men are threatening criminals - an implicit bias.

While implicit bias and racism may feel like one and the same thing, there's a major difference between them. Implicit bias is more covert and racism is mostly overt. Implicit bias isn't generally openly expressed; people don't even realize they have it. Racism on the other hand, consists of openly believing that one race is superior to the other and letting your actions show that.

Racism resides in the top parts of the brain, implicit bias is found deeper in the lower primitive parts.

Thankfully, the cortex is the most malleable part of the brain. So changing one's beliefs and values concerning racism is quite possible. Implicit bias, however, is another story.

One must first recognize that they have implicit bias in order to address it. Eliminating implicit bias requires a person to be more self-aware. It also demands that one experiences different cultures, cuisines and traditions to reverse their biases.

And it requires that we address factors that create implicit bias in the first place.

So we could all be more '*connected*' and more '*human*'.

## Lessons

1. A child is shaped by their environment, good or bad.

2. There's bias both inside and outside us.

3. People affected by bias are also traumatized.

4. Our systems need more experience and training in trauma.

5. Therapy doesn't work without connectedness.

6. The people we grow up with have a huge impact on the racist beliefs and biases we develop.

7. Our racist beliefs can change but implicit bias is hard to recognize and eliminate.

## Issues To Think About

1. The impact of environment on a child

   - Question: Do we shape our environment or does the environment shape us? What do you think?

     _____
     _____
     _____
     _____
     _____

   - Question: What type of environment were you raised in as a child? How did it impact you?

     _____
     _____
     _____
     _____
     _____

2. Trauma-Informed Care (TIC)

- Question: Did you ever experience a situation where you think a more trauma-informed approach would have worked better? Think of your experiences with the hospital, school, law enforcement etc.

_____

_____

_____

_____

_____

3. Racism and implicit bias

- Question: We all have some form of implicit bias and prejudices inside us. Can you point out yours?

_____

_____

_____

_____

_____

- Question: Growing up, what did you think about People of Color or Black people in particular? What factors do you think had the most influence on your thinking?

_____

_____

_____

_____

_____

- Question: Growing up, what did you think about the White people? What factors do you think had the most influence on your thinking?

_____

_____

_____

- Question: What's your experience with racism? How do you think it affects a person's mental health?

_____
_____
_____
_____
_____

4. Therapy without connectedness

- Question: Have you ever felt like you can't get along with anyone? Why do you think it's like that?

_____
_____
_____
_____
_____

- Question: Did you ever go to a therapist? How was your experience?

_____
_____
_____
_____
_____

- Question: Do you think therapy helps with connectedness or connectedness helps with therapy? Please explain why.

_____
_____

_____

_____

_____

## Achieving Targets

1. How can we shape a more positive environment for our kids?

2. How can you apply a more trauma-informed approach to your profession?

3. How can you eliminate your implicit biases? How can you make sure they don't develop in your children?

4. How can you increase your connectedness with a supportive circle of friends, family, relatives, co-workers etc?

## Actionable Movements

1. Included below are a few ways to create a more positive environment for your child at home.

   In the blank space following each, write down how you'll implement them in your own life.

   - How can you be a voice of encouragement, love and patience, support and acceptance for your children?

     _____

     _____

     _____

     _____

   - How can you give proper encouragement to your children?

     _____

     _____

     _____

     _____

- How can you be more affectionate towards your children?

  _____
  _____
  _____
  _____

- How can you model the behavior you want to see in your kids?

  _____
  _____
  _____
  _____

- How can you make your kids feel special every day without going overboard?

  _____
  _____
  _____
  _____

2. Make a list of a trauma-informed school, hospital and police station around you.

   - Trauma-informed school

     _____

   - Trauma-informed hospital

     _____

   - Trauma-informed police station

     _____

3. Included below are a few ways to adapt a trauma-aware approach to any profession.

In the blank space following each, write down how you'll implement them in your professional life.

- Start from here: I'm a —-_____by profession.

- How can you avoid any practices that may be re-traumatizing for the people you interact with in your profession?

  _____
  _____
  _____
  _____

- How can you know who you're serving better?

  _____
  _____
  _____
  _____

- How can you offer more trauma-specific services to the people you serve? (example: offering additional services for the survivors of domestic abuse)

  _____
  _____
  _____
  _____

- How can you be more sensitive to differences in culture, language, ethnicity and race in your work?

  _____
  _____
  _____
  _____

4. Included below are a few ways to expose yourself to cultural diversity.

   In the blank space following each, write down how you'll implement them in your life.

   - How can you make new friends with people from other cultures?

     _____
     _____
     _____
     _____

   - Which movies, books and documentaries can you watch to learn more about other cultures?

     _____
     _____
     _____
     _____

   - How can you travel more (within your city/country or internationally) to interact with people of different cultures?

     _____
     _____
     _____
     _____

   - How can you learn more about your own culture and appreciate the cultural diversity that exists between your culture and other cultures?

     _____
     _____
     _____
     _____

5. Included below are a few ways to ensure that the children around you develop positive early associations regarding people who are different.

   In the blank space following each, write down how you'll implement them in your life.

   - How can you teach them more than one language?

     _____
     _____
     _____
     _____

   - How can you expose your children to different cultural foods and festivities?

     _____
     _____
     _____
     _____

   - How can you encourage your children to make friends with children from other cultures?

     _____
     _____
     _____
     _____

   - How can you be the perfect role model for your kids to help them accept cultural diversity?

     _____
     _____
     _____
     _____

6. Take this free test by Project Implicit which is a non-profit organization helping people identify their hidden biases. ( https://implicit.harvard.edu/implicit/ )

Then complete the following steps.

- Write down the findings of your test below

_____

_____

_____

_____

_____

- Assess where or when these biases are most likely to affect your perception?

_____

_____

_____

_____

_____

- How can you make some changes in your life to consciously eliminate these biases?

_____

_____

_____

_____

_____

## Checklist

1. The environment you grew up in has a great impact on you.

2. Recognize, accept and try to change your implicit biases and prejudices. We all have them.

3. Before seeking therapy, make sure you're well-connected with a supportive circle of people around you.

# Chapter Nine – Relational Hunger In The Modern World

## <u>Summary</u>

*" The collective 'We' of a community heals. 'We' are all healers."*

*-Dr. Perry*

Connectedness has an overpowering healing effect.

It was Dr. Perry's interactions with indigenous communities and their healers that helped him realize he was missing an important aspect of patient care: relational health. He wasn't asking his patients things like 'How do they spend their day?' or 'Who are their best friends?' or 'Do they have any best friends at all?'.

He wasn't getting to the heart of pain, distress and dysfunction; *connectedness.*

Connectedness, as we've also talked about earlier, refers to reciprocal and family relationships that invoke a sense of connection and belonging.

Unfortunately, the modern world severely lacks connectedness.

This has a direct impact on our resilience against everyday stressors; Less connectedness means lesser buffering capacity.

As a result, we're becoming increasingly vulnerable to small challenges. We're threatened at the slightest indication and have lost the tolerance to consider and reflect on others' point of view.

But miscommunication and conflict is also the essence of all human communication. It is through having an argument, and thereafter making repairs, that the stress-response system becomes more resilient. Miscommunication therefore provides a moderate but vital dose of stressors.

*True growth springs from tough moments when you have a conflict or difficult conversation with someone and resolve the situation with empathy.*

We have a conflict. We repair the damage. We reconnect and grow.

Being empathic in a tense situation has a huge impact on one's responses. And that, in turn, changes everything. When you try to understand the feelings of the other person and how they might be viewing the situation, you get to know them better and be more regulated in how you deal with them.

And that's important..

Because the modern human lives in a very different world than their ancestors.

It used to be that 99.9% of the time of our existence was spent in small hunter-gatherer groups, nestled deeply within nature. Each of us only knew about 60-100 people at a time and there was more physical proximity and connectedness with those that we knew.

Compared to that, we now live in a strange world.

Consider a person living in the city, for example. This person's stress-response system is extremely fatigued due to continuous monitoring of the thousands of stimuli around them. There are new faces, sights, sounds and smells all around. They're also fighting against nature; eating processed foods and using artificial lighting, while simultaneously worrying about housing, food, taxes and employment.

All of this is extremely stressful to their brain and body.

Modern life is also messed up because it doesn't support relational interactions. Resultantly, we've lost a rich source of regulation, reward and learning; the transgenerational multifamily clans. What we now have is more screen-time than family-time.

Consequently, neither we nor our children have the same capacity for storytelling, learning or communication. We're also less empathic because we lack the opportunities for caring relational interactions. So it's only natural that we have more issues with intimacy, social skills and interpersonal behavior.

*You can't love if you've never been loved.*

You can't communicate if you've never been communicated with. And you can't empathize if you've never been empathized with.

The latest cultural shift promotes more 'extrinsic' and 'materialistic' goals. There have also been some major changes in our family structure. Sadly, these *innovations* have resulted in more loneliness and disconnection leading to problems like anxiety, sleep issues, depression and substance use.

In fact, it won't be wrong to say that the current state of a person's mental health is a direct representative of their relational health.

Disconnection is a painful disease. And while this pain is expressed differently by everyone, it originates from one place only i.e. relational poverty.

Connectedness is even more, if not as important, in determining a person's mental health than their history of trauma. Sadly, this doesn't prevent us from raising our children in relationally poor environments. Add in the fact that we now prefer to tweet and post instead of having actual conversations and the situation is even more bleak.

But when these superficial interactions on social media don't satisfy us, we feel emptier and seek connection in other unhealthy ways.

The above is true whether a person is rich or poor. In fact, poverty is an even bigger trigger for disconnectedness because poor finances lead to marginalization, which ultimately makes one feel that they don't belong. This activates their stress-response system and makes them feel even more disconnected than before.

The dilemma of connectedness is worse in urban areas. When someone living in a city encounters hundreds of new people every day, their natural response is ignorance. That's because it's tough on the brain to evaluate each and every individual to assess if they're friends or foe. Combine this with thousands of other stimuli that this person encounters in a busy city and you know where their anxiety is coming from.

It takes time and energy to know someone or someplace new. And we only have a certain amount of mental disk space available. So we often disconnect and immerse ourselves in our devices. Where we find nothing but hollow connections and even more isolation.

Isolation can be traumatic because it can sensitize the stress-response system. Relational poverty is, therefore, a form of adversity particularly for our children.

This might be a hard pill for most to swallow. After all, our children seem to have everything we never had. But the reality says that they are starving from a lack of connectedness, despite all their possessions.

Children need many forms of nourishment, one of which is healthy touch. While most of us are aware and wary of bad touch, we fail to recognize that there are ways to allow healthy touch while protecting the children. It is developmentally ignorant to give children toys or a screen instead of holding them with affection. Particularly since we're just beginning to understand the impact of screen-time on the developing brain.

Speaking of screen-time, Dr. Perry believes that we're inventing technology at a faster pace than we can understand its impact on our lives. He therefore suggests that we should develop some 'social-practice' rules regarding the use of technology. For instance, introducing 'no-phone zones' and a proper 'dosing' of screen-time for individuals of different ages.

He calls these *'techno-hygiene'* measures which are meant to ensure that our use of technology remains in check. This is particularly important for children under the age of 2-3 years who shouldn't even be looking at a screen or tablet. Instead, in an ideal world, they should be exploring the world around them using all of their sensory tools.

A child raised in a relationally rich environment with ample opportunities for safe and nurturing interactions will develop strong resilience. They'll have the empathy to meaningfully connect with others, thereby healing themselves and those around them.

Because, as said in the beginning of this chapter, the *collective 'We' of a community heals. 'We' are all healers.*

## Lessons

1.  Healing is connectedness and connectedness is healing.

2. We're becoming increasingly vulnerable because we're more connected to our phones than people.

3. It's normal to have conflict and miscommunication. Managing these effectively helps us grow and have better relationships.

4. Modern lifestyle is extremely stressful for our brain and body. It's also more isolating.

5. Anxiety, depression, sleep issues and substance use are often the result of isolation and disconnection.

6. Our children are starving for healthy touch and affection.

## Issues To Think About

1. Connectedness

   - Question: Do you feel well-connected with friends, family, relatives and other people in your life? Why or why not?

     _____
     _____
     _____
     _____
     _____

   - Question: Have you ever felt the healing power of connectedness in your life? Can you recall what happened?

     _____
     _____
     _____
     _____
     _____

2. Conflict management

- Question: Do you consider yourself good at conflict management? Why or why not?

_____
_____
_____
_____
_____

- Question: Do you think conflict management is hard to learn? Why or why not?

_____
_____
_____
_____
_____

3. Modern lifestyle and the use of social media

- Question: What are some drawbacks of modern life that you've personally experienced?

_____
_____
_____
_____

- Question: What do you think is the biggest drawback of an 'Online life'? Why?

_____
_____
_____
_____

- Question: Do you think modern lifestyle is making us lonely? Why or why not?

_____
_____

_____
_____

- Question: Why do you think we're more anxious and depressed than our ancestors?

  _____
  _____
  _____
  _____

4. Use of technology and screen time

   - Question: Which type of screen time do you or your children engage in more? Do you think it's a healthy amount of screen time?

     _____
     _____
     _____

5. Healthy touch

   - Question: How much do you know about healthy touch and safe, respectable ways to interact with your children?

     _____
     _____
     _____
     _____

   - Question: Do you think adults need training about how to balance children's needs for warmth and affection with safe, respectful ways of interacting? Why?

     _____
     _____
     _____
     _____

## Achieving Targets

1. How to find ways to be more connected with friends, family and co-workers?

2. How to raise our children so they grow up to be more empathic?

3. How to learn conflict-management at work, home and with friends?

4. How to limit our screen-time and make more connections out of social media?

5. How can we learn to provide our children with safe and respectable forms of physical affection?

## Actionable Movements

1. Complete the following table to know if you're really connecting with others. The first one has been done for you as an example.

| When connecting with others, you feel... | Yes | No | Please explain your answer |
|---|---|---|---|
| You're in the moment | | ✓ | I always feel like I'm thinking about what went wrong in the past or worrying about future |
| You're being yourself | | | |
| You're open to share both good and bad stuff | | | |
| You're empathic and kind towards them | | | |

| You have a sense of trust between you | | | |
|---|---|---|---|
| | | | |

2.  Take the following examples of human connection. Write down how they might apply to your life. The first one has been done for you as an example.

- Taking the time to listen to someone else and feeling real empathy for them
  The next time I'm talking to my partner, I'll make sure that I don't just plan what to say next. Instead, I'll simply be present to what they're saying.

- Helping someone else out of unconditional goodwill

  _____

  _____

  _____

  _____

- Offering sincere gratitude to another and receiving gratitude from others

  _____

  _____

  _____

  _____

- Enjoying a shared experience with others that involves laughter and goodwill

  _____

  _____

  _____

  _____

- Having a personal conversation about what is important to you with someone and feeling listened to and understood

_____

_____

_____

_____

3. Write down the biggest and most common conflicts you have with your family, friends and at work. Explore 1-2 ways to manage each of these effectively.

- My biggest conflict with family is

_____

_____

I plan to resolve this conflict effectively by

_____

_____

_____

- My biggest conflict with friend(s) is

_____

_____

I plan to resolve this conflict effectively by

_____

_____

_____

- My biggest conflict at work is

_____

_____

I plan to resolve this conflict effectively by

_____

_____

_____

4. Included below are 5 ways to develop empathy in your kids.

In the blank space following each, write down how you'll implement these in your kids' life.

- How can you empathize more with your child?

  _____
  _____
  _____

- How can you talk about others' feelings in front of them?

  _____
  _____
  _____

- How can you practice random acts of kindness towards others alongside them?

  _____
  _____
  _____

- How can you model empathy for them in other everyday situations?

  _____
  _____
  _____

5. Search online to find out how much screen time is appropriate for you and/or your children. Compare it with your approximate current screen time.

   - Appropriate screen time for me —-_____.

   - I spent approximately — _____ hours in front of a screen.

   - Appropriate screen time for my children by age — _____

- My child spends approximately — _____ hours in front of a screen.

6. Explore 3 ways to ban excess screen time for yourself and your family (example: I'll have no-phone zones around the house)

- #1

_____
_____

- #2

_____
_____

- #3

_____
_____

7. Explore 3 ways in which you can make loving and caring touch part of your child's daily routine (example: I'll practice giving more hugs to my child, asking them if they prefer a tight squeeze or a gentle squeeze)

- #1

_____
_____

- #2

_____
_____

- #3

_____
_____

8. To help them understand the difference between good touch and bad touch as well as empower them about their bodies, here are some books you can read to your children;

- **Book #1** Some Secrets Should Never Be Kept by Jayneen Sanders, illustrated by Craig Smith

- **Book #2** My Body Belongs to Me by Jill Starishevsky

- **Book #3** It's Not the Stork! by Robie H. Harris

## Checklist

1. Connectedness is a basic human need.

2. Conflict management may be tough, but like all tough things, it helps us grow.

3. More often than not, an isolated person ends up being depressed or anxious. They may also develop sleep troubles or resort to substance use to fill the emptiness inside them.

4. Children need physical affection and love more than they need fancy toys.

# Chapter 10 – What We Need Now

## Summary

*" It really is never too late. Healing is always possible"*

-Dr. Perry

Trauma-awareness has come a long way.

Along the journey, a neurosequential approach to helping the traumatized has been a milestone.

The Neurosequential Model developed by Dr. Perry and his team is based on an important idea; the brain develops, processes sensory input, and heals, *in a sequence*.

Everything in our brain is *'Neurosequential'*.

The Neurosequential Model therefore addresses the brain's problems in a proper sequence. This means that any problems originating in the lower parts of the brain are addressed first before moving on to the more 'sophisticated' problems pertaining to higher parts of the brain.

The Neurosequential model also accounts for 'state-dependent' functioning of the brain. We've discussed state-dependent functioning before; depending on what state you're in (calm, vigilance, alarm, fear or terror), different parts of the brain are activated. The model allows a person to assess whether a person is in a state where they'll be able to hear and understand what someone else might be saying to them.

In other words, are they in a state to be reasoned with?

A neurosequential approach can be of immense help to anyone dealing with a child; teachers, parents and clinicians. It can do wonders when a child's developmental capabilities are far behind their actual age or when they're in a state of fear unable to benefit from conventional 'teaching', 'coaching' or 'reasoning'.

This isn't to say that traditional therapeutic methods don't work. A neurosequential model uses many of these conventional treatment methods. But it does so at a *proper time* and in *a proper sequence*.

The bottom line being; no matter *What Happened to You*, it's possible to change things for the better.

*It really is never too late, healing is always possible.*

What's critical to healing is to know from where to start the process and match the developmental needs of the person. It also helps to understand trauma and its impact and how the brain works.

That's the first step on the path to healing; recognizing that you're not bad or stupid or simply unlucky. It's just that your brain is organized differently based on *What Happened to You*. And since the brain is malleable like plastic, with some help, you can change the patterns and systems that are causing you problems.

This will allow you to regulate yourself and to do the work you're supposed to do in a way that's admirable, to say the least.

Because an unregulated parent can't raise a child properly, an unregulated employee can't perform well at work and an unregulated spouse can't make their partner feel loved and appreciated.

We must take care of ourselves to bring out the best in us and to help regulate those in our care and responsibility.

And while adversity is an undeniable part of this world, it isn't necessarily bad. It helps us develop the capacity to be empathic and become wise. Post-traumatic wisdom is real and can only be achieved once you own your trauma and claim it.

The wounds of your past will continue to bleed until you face them squarely and heal yourself.

All of this isn't to say that post-traumatic wisdom comes without a cost. But trauma is, nonetheless, a precious gift. What we do with this gift is up to us, both individually and as a society. Just like it's important to know *What Happened to You* as an individual, it's vital for a society to confront its historical trauma to embrace a more humane, just, creative and productive future.

Our world isn't a hopeless place, regardless of all the adversity found within. We're a curious species that has evolved to discover, learn and invent to make its future better than the past.

And by learning to discover, embrace and grow from our individual and collective trauma, we can make it an even better place.

## Lessons

1. It's possible to heal from a traumatic past and learn to carry your pain with grace.

2. The brain works in a sequence. This is why a neurosequential model of treatment works best to help a traumatized person.

3. You're not crazy, stupid, or lazy. Your feelings are caused by what you've been through.

4. Self-care isn't being selfish. You can't regulate or take care of somebody else if you aren't regulated yourself.

5. Trauma can make us wise and more empathic.

## Issues To Think About

1. Healing from trauma

   - Question: Do you think we can heal from trauma? Why or why not?

   _____
   _____
   _____
   _____
   _____

   - Question: Have you ever used a method/technique to help yourself heal from trauma? How successful were you in doing so?

_____
_____
_____
_____
_____

2. Validating emotions

- Question: How do you validate your emotions?

_____
_____
_____
_____
_____

- Question: How does it feel to validate someone else's emotions? Do you feel compelled to agree with them?

_____
_____
_____
_____
_____

3. Importance of self-care

- Question: What are your views about self-care? Do you think it's important?

_____
_____
_____
_____
_____

- Question: What do you think is the biggest obstacle in taking care of yourself? How successfully do you overcome it?

_____

_____

_____

_____

_____

4. Post-traumatic wisdom

- Question: What do you understand by the term 'post-traumatic wisdom'? How do you think it is achieved?

_____

_____

_____

_____

_____

- Question: Have you ever felt 'wiser' after a traumatic event? How was that?

_____

_____

_____

_____

_____

## Achieving Targets

1. How to heal yourself after trauma?

2. How to better take care of yourself and think more positively about yourself?

3. How to own your trauma and get something good out of it?

4. How to be more wise and empathic in the wake of trauma?

# Actionable Movements

1. Below are 5 ways to help heal from trauma.

   In the blank space following each, write down how they might apply to your life.

   The first one has been done for you as an example.

   - Connect with others - I'll try to spend some time with my friends when I feel like it.

   - Physical movement –

     _____

     _____

   - Practicing self-care –

     _____

     _____

   - Taking breaks –

     _____

     _____

   - Engaging in creativity –

     _____

     _____

2. Fill in the blanks below and write a validating statement about how you're feeling right now

   " I understand that I'm feeling —-_____ today. I can see why I might be feeling that way.
   It's because — _____."

   Use this statement whenever you're feeling emotionally overwhelmed to better understand your emotions.

3. Included below are 5 different types of self-care for your mind and body.

In the blank space following each, write down how you'll implement these in your life.

The first one has been done for you as an example.

- Physical self-care (take care of your body) - I'll make sure to get 7 hours of good-quality sleep each night.

- Social self-care (self-care through socialization) –

  _____
  _____

- Mental self-care (taking care of your mind) –

  _____
  _____

- Spiritual self-care (taking care of your soul) –

  _____
  _____

- Emotional self-care (taking care of your emotions) –

  _____
  _____

4. Complete the following exercise to help unlock post-traumatic wisdom in your life.

   Feel free to be as candid as possible.

   - What are some personal strengths that you've always possessed in life? Skills that you had even before your traumatic experience.

     _____
     _____
     _____
     _____

_____

_____

- Which of these strengths have helped you cope with the trauma effectively?

_____

_____

_____

_____

_____

_____

- What new strengths do you think you've acquired as a result of your traumatic experience?

_____

_____

_____

_____

_____

_____

- How do you think your life philosophy has changed as a result?

_____

_____

_____

_____

_____

_____

## Checklist

1. It's possible to reverse the impact of trauma on your life.

2. You are the way you are because of _What Happened to You._

3.  Taking care of yourself and being selfish aren't the same things.

4.  Trauma is a gift. It rewards you with wisdom and empathy.

5.  Learning about What Happened to You is as important for a society as it is for an individual.

# Now It's Your Turn

## In Depth Exercises

Complete the following exercises and answer the questions in as much detail as possible.

*One*

Rewrite the following statement in the space below, making any changes according to your own situation;

"I understand that I'm not crazy, stupid, lazy or incompetent. I think and behave like this because of *What Happened to Me*"

_____

_____

_____

*Two*

Now think back to a time when you had trauma visited upon you or you witnessed trauma happening to someone else. Try to describe what happened in as much detail as possible.

_____

_____

_____

_____

_____

_____

_____

_____

_____

_____

_____

*Three*

Can you recall how long ago this happened? Why or why not?

_Four_

What did you feel at the time? What are your feelings now that you're recalling the event?

_Five_

If this was your personal trauma, do you have a friend, family member or coworker who experienced something similar? How did they cope with it?

*Six*

Have you completed all the exercises in this workbook?

If that's not the case, please go back and take your time to complete all the exercises in this workbook and then continue this exercise.

*Seven*

How do you feel now that you've read this workbook and completed all the exercises?

_____

_____

_____

_____

_____

_____

_____

_____

_____

_____

*Eight*

What do you think has made the biggest difference in your thinking about trauma and its impacts after reading this workbook?

_____

_____

_____

_____

_____

_____

_____

_____

_____

_____

*Nine*

If there is just one thing that stuck with you after reading this workbook, what's that? Why do you think it stuck with you?

_____
_____
_____
_____
_____
_____
_____
_____
_____
_____

*Ten*

How do you think you'll deal with your trauma after reading this workbook? How is this different from what you would have done before reading the workbook?

_____
_____
_____
_____
_____
_____
_____
_____
_____

# Author's Note

Thank you for taking the time to read this workbook and answer all the questions and exercises within. I hope that you now have a better understanding of how *What Happened to You* has impacted your life and leave this workbook with a newfound appreciation for the good and bad of adversity.

I wish you all the happiness and success in this world.

May *What Happened to You* become your greatest gift ever!

And may you find peace and happiness along your journey in life.

Made in the USA
Las Vegas, NV
30 October 2022